Microsoft Press

Introducing
Microsoft
Windows 2000
Server

Anthony Northrup

PUBLISHED BY
Microsoft Press
A Division of Microsoft Corporation
One Microsoft Way
Redmond, Washington 98052-6399

Library of Congress Cataloging-in-Publication Data
Northrup, Tony.
    Introducing Microsoft Windows 2000 Server / Tony Northrup
        p.   cm.
    ISBN 1-57231-875-9
    1. Microsoft Windows 2000 server.   2. Operating systems
(Computers)   I. Northrup, Tony.   II. Title.
QA76.76.063N6745   1999
005.4'469--dc21   99-13557
                                                            CIP

Printed and bound in the United States of America.

1 2 3 4 5 6 7 8 9   MLML   4 3 2 1 0 9

Distributed in Canada by Penguin Books Canada Limited.

A CIP catalogue record for this book is available from the British Library.

Microsoft Press books are available through booksellers and distributors worldwide. For further information about international editions, contact your local Microsoft Corporation office or contact Microsoft Press International directly at fax (425) 936-7329. Visit our Web site at mspress.microsoft.com.

Acquisitions Editor: Juliana Aldous
Project Editor: Maureen Williams Zimmerman
Technical Editor: Jean Ross

For my dad.

CONTENTS

PART IV: DISTRIBUTED SERVICES

CHAPTER NINE

Overview of Distributed Services **121**

CHAPTER TEN

The Microsoft Distributed File System (Dfs)   **137**

CHAPTER ELEVEN

Active Directory   **143**

CHAPTER TWELVE

Preparing for Windows 2000 Server   **165**

ACKNOWLEDGEMENTS

It takes many people to write a book, and each person who helped has my gratitude. The crew at Microsoft Press is the best I've ever worked with. I worked most closely with Maureen Zimmerman, Anne Hamilton, and Juliana Aldous, but I thank everyone who worked on this book.

My friends and family have always supported me. Thanks go to my mother, my father, and the rest of my family. Many others helped me relieve the elevated stress—especially Erica Edson, Peter Aquaman, Ari Globerman, Chris Russo, Kurt Dillard, Stephanie Wunderlich, Bill Duffy, Raymond Lamm, DJ Eric John Parucki, Todd Wesche, and Tara Banks. Finally, a very special thanks to Dr. Anthony Erdmann and his *Ginkgo biloba*.

INTRODUCTION

Computer networking is the fastest growing industry ever. Software and hardware vendors continuously develop new technologies to keep up with demand from customers.

Microsoft has made itself successful in a very competitive market by listening to its customers and meeting their needs. Microsoft Windows 2000 Server is the result of several years of interacting with systems engineers to determine what features their organizations most need in a network operating system.

One of the challenges of being a systems engineer is keeping up with these new technologies. They have been created for your benefit, but learning about them and learning how to implement them can be time consuming.

This book has been written to introduce you to Windows 2000 Server. I hope it will save you time and save your company money. This book is an excellent resource for experienced systems administrators, even those who have already mastered Microsoft Windows NT. It is also intended for readers who are entirely new to Windows networking. Simply put, with this book you will understand Windows 2000 Server.

The Evolution of Microsoft's Server Software

In the beginning, there was LAN Manager. This product provided part of the foundation of Windows NT 3.1 Advanced Server. Windows NT 3.1 Advanced Server shared the same user interface and many of the same applications as Windows 3.1, but it had a powerful set of networking features. With it, systems engineers had an operating system reliable enough to depend on for important network services, such as file and print sharing.

LAN Manager provided a user-friendly alternative to UNIX and Novell NetWare that suited small-sized to medium-sized networks. Windows NT 3.1 and LAN Manager did not quickly saturate the market, however. Companies depend on their networks to support their business and generally do not make major changes easily.

Windows NT Server 3.5 and 3.51 continued the evolution and became common additions to networks of all sizes. Near the end of the product life cycle, Microsoft released a free add-on called Internet Information Server 1.0. This software ushered Windows NT into UNIX territory: the Internet.

Windows NT Server 4.0 was an improved operating system, especially in its Internet capabilities. The TCP/IP protocol stack was greatly improved, DNS services were offered, and Internet Information Server was greatly enhanced as version 2.0.

The next step in the evolution of Microsoft server software is the largest, and the one this book is dedicated to describing—Windows 2000 Server. In this introduction, I'll walk you through the features of the software and show you where you can find more information.

An Overview of Windows 2000 Features

A lot of the momentum of computer networking is driven by the rapid growth of the Internet. Windows NT Server claimed 23 percent of the Internet Web server market and 70 percent of the intranet server market during 1998.

Internet Information Services 5.0 is included with Windows 2000, and it features many improvements geared specifically toward Internet service providers who offer Web hosting services. Among other advancements, it now supports HTTP compression, virtual server processor quotas, and process accounting.

NOTE: You'll learn more about Internet Information Services in Chapter 8.

Most end users are less interested in the operating system and far more excited by the applications software that supports their daily work or play. The key to providing applications to users is attracting the attention of the developers. Ninety-one percent of all software developers now provide, or plan to provide soon, software that runs on Windows NT and Windows 2000. UNIX developers are recognizing this trend as well—50 percent of Sun Solaris developers are now targeting the Windows NT platform for their products.

Microsoft's Component Object Model (COM) technology is responsible for attracting many developers. COM is now woven into just about every aspect of Microsoft's own software—operating systems, development tools, and applications. Ultimately, COM benefits both administrators *and* developers because it allows applications to be distributed on the network and updated centrally.

NOTE: You'll read more about these capabilities in Chapters 4 and 11.

The most important addition to Windows 2000 is Active Directory. It allows any user or application to locate any available network resource. It stores more than the location of objects; it stores critical information about the object. For example, a user's name, phone number, and address are all stored within

Active Directory and can be retrieved by anyone with proper access to the network. Many of Windows 2000 Server's network services store information within Active Directory to take advantage of its distributed, reliable nature. A resource as critical as Active Directory must be running at all times. Thanks to the fact that you can run the service on many machines simultaneously, it can be.

NOTE: Find more information about Active Directory in Chapter 11.

Windows 2000 will make your file servers more reliable and efficient than ever with the new Microsoft distributed file system (Dfs). Dfs allows shares to be mirrored between file servers and enables clients to automatically choose the closest server. Ultimately, Dfs will reduce network traffic, increase uptime, and improve the load distribution between your servers.

NOTE: Chapter 10 describes Dfs in detail.

Windows 2000 Server includes strong storage capabilities. The addition of the NTFS 5 file system allows for greater expandability than was available in previous versions of Windows. Disk quotas have also been included in Windows 2000. New backup utilities make backup and recovery easier and more reliable.

NOTE: For more on storage and backup, see Chapter 2.

Users will never lose access to their most critical network documents, applications, and desktop settings—thanks to IntelliMirror. Windows 2000 systems can keep duplicate copies of important information on the client and the server. If the user loses access to the server, he or she can keep working on a network document because Windows 2000 will automatically use the locally cached copy. When the server is restored, updates are automatically synchronized. IntelliMirror also copies data from desktop systems to servers, enabling users to move from one computer to another and have the same desktop settings, applications, and documents available.

NOTE: IntelliMirror, as well as the other Zero Administration for Windows technologies, are described in Chapter 3.

Administering a network of Windows 2000 systems will be easier and faster than ever because of the Microsoft Management Console (MMC). The MMC gives you control over which tools and computers are displayed, allowing you to create custom administration tools catered to your specific responsibilities. User Manager, Event View, Server Manager, Disk Administrator, and all other administrative applications have been rewritten as MMC snap-ins. Experienced administrators will quickly adapt to the new tools; new administrators will learn faster thanks to the consistent, user-friendly interface. I have described each of these new tools in this book.

The new WMI (Windows Management Instrumentation) standards will make large, heterogeneous networks simpler to manage. WMI provides applications with an interface to monitoring and managing systems, similar to the capabilities currently provided by SNMP. If your network is entirely Windows-based, you might never have to use WMI. For those who administer a combination of Windows 2000 systems and UNIX systems, WMI will allow your enterprise management applications to interface with every system on your network.

NOTE: Chapter 4 has a wealth of information about WMI.

Managing desktop environments will be easier than ever thanks to Group Policy and Active Directory. You can now grant and restrict user and group access to various aspects of Windows 2000, such as applications, desktop settings, network access, and the Start menu. Policies exist within Active Directory and can be quickly applied to an entire enterprise. Additionally, users and groups within the enterprise can have specialized settings that meet their specific needs.

NOTE: Learn about policy management in Chapter 3.

Administrators do not need to maintain a separate set of drivers for Windows 2000 and Microsoft Windows 98 systems because of the introduction of the Windows Driver Model (WDM). Merging the drivers for the two operating systems brings us one step closer to the next generation of Windows, when home and business operating systems will be merged.

Further, Windows 2000 completely supports Plug and Play and the advanced power management capabilities of Advanced Configuration and Power Interface (ACPI). These features will reduce the time you spend working with your server hardware. In most cases, the operating system will automatically detect and configure new hardware as soon as you add it.

NOTE: Chapter 1 describes low-level changes to Windows 2000, including Plug and Play, WDM, ACPI, and OnNow.

Security is an ongoing concern in computing, and it is especially vital in network systems. Windows 2000 Server includes one of the strongest security systems to date. It provides built-in support for certification authorities and smart cards, as well as the standards-based Kerberos authentication protocol.

NOTE: Learn more about network security in Windows 2000 Server in Chapter 5.

International users will benefit from Windows 2000's globalization effort. Globalization allows developers to create a single application that can work in any environment, regardless of the language, keyboard layout, and other locale-specific settings. This is not a new initiative within Microsoft. Unicode, which allows any language to be stored and represented, was built into the first version of Windows NT.

NOTE: Read Chapter 1 to learn what makes Windows 2000 a truly worldwide operating system.

As networks grow, network systems need to scale upward as well. Modern network applications are more powerful than ever and demand more of the server hardware. Windows 2000 is ready for these intensive applications with its improved support for multiple processors, huge amounts of memory, highly scalable file systems, and clustering. Windows 2000 Server comes in three variations depending on your scalability needs: Server, Advanced Server, and Datacenter Server. Datacenter Server, the most powerful of the Windows 2000 Server family of operating systems, represents Microsoft's best effort to compete in the high-end server market.

The network connectivity capabilities have been expanded as well. Windows 2000 is ready to participate in IP telephony, a technology that will merge data and voice networks. L2TP (Layer 2 Tunneling Protocol), PPTP (Point-to-Point Tunneling Protocol), and IPSec (Internet Protocol security) integrate virtual private networking into the operating system, allowing the Internet to be used to transport any type of private data. The improved switching capabilities enable Windows 2000 to play a new role—that of a network router. Streaming media is now a viable technology, thanks to new support for Quality of Service (QoS) standards and the integration of Windows Media Services (formerly NetShow) into Windows 2000 Server.

NOTE: The new networking features of Windows 2000 Server are described in Chapter 6. Chapter 7 covers Windows Media Services.

Besides having newly polished MMC administrative interfaces, the core TCP/IP network services have all been improved and updated. Domain Name System (DNS) now supports the DNS dynamic update protocol. Windows Internet Name Service (WINS) offers persistent replication connections and improved redundancy. Dynamic Host Configuration Protocol (DHCP) is integrated with DNS dynamic update protocol, and Windows 2000 DHCP clients will now boot successfully even in the absence of a DHCP server.

NOTE: To learn more about DNS, WINS, and DHCP, skip to Chapter 9.

This book will guide you through implementing and upgrading to Windows 2000. Whether your network is small or large, you will learn the steps necessary to plan a successful migration project. You will understand how much time to schedule, what factors will go into creating a budget, and how to test Windows 2000 in your environment.

> **NOTE:** To learn about implementing Windows 2000 Server, read Chapter 12.

I hope you enjoy reading this book. More important, I hope it provides you with the information you need to get started with Windows 2000 Server. If you have any comments or questions, feel free to contact me at northrup@ultranet.com.

Support

Every effort has been made to ensure the accuracy of this book. Microsoft Press provides corrections for books through the World Wide Web at the following address:

http://mspress.microsoft.com/mspress/support/

If you have comments, questions, or ideas regarding this book, please send them to Microsoft Press using either of the following methods:

Postal Mail:
Microsoft Press
Attn: *Introducing Microsoft Windows 2000 Server* Editor
One Microsoft Way
Redmond, WA 98052-6399

E-mail:
MSPINPUT@MICROSOFT.COM

Please note that product support is not offered through the above mail addresses. For more information regarding Windows 2000, you can check Microsoft's Web site:

http://www.microsoft.com/windows

BASE SERVICES

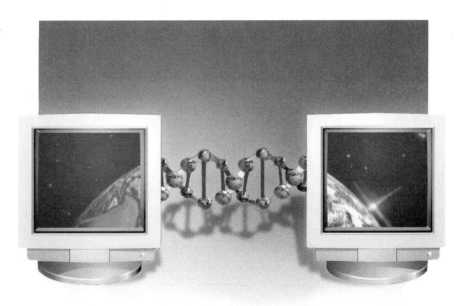

The Microsoft Windows 2000 Server Kernel

Evolution of the Kernel Architecture

Microsoft Windows 2000 is composed of many different layers that all interact to present the user with a complete operating system. At the core of this architecture lies the kernel. The kernel is not just another process running on the system; it has special rights over the hardware of the system. The kernel is responsible for allocating memory to applications, for communicating with device drivers, and for determining which processes run at any given time.

Applications depend on the kernel to allocate memory, processor time, and hardware resources. The Windows 2000 Server kernel has evolved directly from the Microsoft Windows NT 4.0 kernel. The Windows NT 4.0 kernel derived from previous versions of Windows NT, as illustrated in Figure 1-1. Each new version was created to meet the changing needs of users, administrators, and developers.

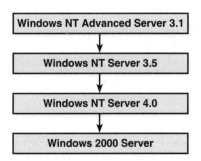

Figure 1-1.
Microsoft Windows 2000 Server is the result of several generations of evolution.

Historically, when application developers have needed functionality that the kernel did not offer, Microsoft has changed the kernel to meet their needs. For example, processor quotas and process accounting have been added specifically to accommodate Internet Information Services 5.0 (IIS). The kernel now provides better multiuser support to allow Terminal Services to be installed without requiring major system changes. Developers benefit because they can now add in much-needed functionality. And, ultimately, administrators and users will benefit from these same changes.

Microsoft has also changed several aspects of the kernel specifically to meet administrators' needs. Among other improvements, Windows 2000 Server now scales much higher than was possible with Windows NT. Network applications are more reliable and run more efficiently than ever before. Users in other countries will have an easier time using the operating system and its applications in their environments.

It is important to understand the changes that have taken place in the kernel before moving on to learn how the various services have been improved. Indeed, many of the improvements to services depend on modifications to the kernel.

Processor Quotas and Accounting

It is common practice for Internet Service Providers (ISPs) to share a single Web server between many customers. Until now, one customer's Web site could dominate the system's processors and degrade the performance of other customers. Similarly, one user's problematic ASP code could render an entire intranet server useless. While IIS provided bandwidth throttling, the operating system was not capable of efficiently controlling how much processor time each Web site received.

Two new features make multiuser environments more effective: processor accounting and CPU throttling. *Processor accounting* is used by IIS to record the number of processor cycles consumed by individual Web requests. This allows ISPs to bill based on processor usage, and enables developers to determine which pages can most benefit from optimization. *CPU throttling* stops a Web site's out-of-process applications from stealing so much processor time that the other Web sites cannot function correctly.

The *job object* is the underlying technology that enables processor accounting and CPU throttling. To understand what a job object does, you should understand how applications and services use processes. Services such as IIS spawn many processes so that multiple tasks can be accomplished at the same time. While multiple processes improve performance, they make it complicated to track which processes are associated with which tasks. Because IIS 4 supported many virtual servers sharing the same application space, it was impossible to audit or control how much processor resources each virtual server consumed.

Job objects allow the operating system to manage groups of processes as a single unit. This makes it much easier for applications to monitor and throttle the amount of processor time that separate tasks consume. This feature is critical for environments where multiple customers share the same server.

NOTE: Simply put, one or more processes can work together to complete a single *job,* which is represented by a job object.

Spin Count

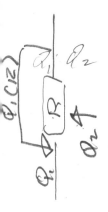

Spin count is a method for improving performance on multiprocessor systems when multiple programs need access to the same resources simultaneously. Spin count controls how many times a process will attempt to access a resource before waiting. To clarify this, consider a database application that has multiple queries running simultaneously on different processors. Query #1 attempts to write to a row of a particular table but is refused access because Query #2 has that row locked. Without spin count, Query #1 would wait a while, blocking execution of the query. With spin count, Query #1 would simply try to write to the row a few times in the hope that Query #2 will release it quickly, and wait only if all attempts are refused.

This only helps on multiprocessor systems because on those systems multiple processes can run simultaneously. On a single processor system, the different processes will have to wait for each other to execute anyway, in which case repeated attempts to access the resource will *not* be successful until the other process has a chance to execute. Applications that use spin count on single processor systems will not hurt their performance; they just will not benefit.

Scatter/Gather I/O

Scatter/Gather I/O is a new feature in Windows 2000 Server that will improve the performance of application servers on your network. Its use is entirely transparent to system administrators, because applications can make use of it without any special configuration. The technology streamlines the process of moving data from discontiguous sections of the system's RAM to a contiguous space on the disk drive. Applications must be written specifically to take advantage of it. Therefore, existing services will not realize any benefit.

This technology was first introduced in Windows NT as part of a service pack, and was specifically intended to improve the performance of Microsoft SQL Server. Windows 2000 Server is the first Microsoft operating system to provide this technology as an included feature.

Waitable Timers

A *quantum* is a property of a thread that defines how long that thread will be allowed to execute before control is handed over to another thread. Administrators and developers now have greater control over quantum type and length. It takes time to switch the CPU between multiple threads, so some applications benefit from increasing the thread quantum length. On the other hand, increasing a thread's time slice makes multitasking less smooth. IG BOTTLENECKS

The quantum type can also be adjusted between fixed length and variable length. This can be configured from the Performance Options dialog box (shown in Figure 1-2), which is accessed from the Advanced tab of the System Properties dialog box. Giving priority to applications allocates short, variable quanta, providing smoother multitasking. Giving priority to background services causes the operating system to use long, fixed quanta, which improves performance of network services. By default, Windows 2000 Server gives priority to background services, and Windows 2000 Professional gives priority to applications.

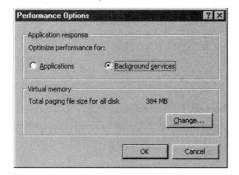

Figure 1-2.
The administrator can now configure quantum type and length.

Windows Driver Model

A *driver* is a piece of software that allows the operating system to communicate with a piece of hardware. Different video cards have different capabilities and different ways of communicating; the driver performs the translation between Windows 2000 and the video card itself. All hardware accessories require drivers: network cards, SCSI cards, modems, scanners, and printers. Previous versions of Windows required different drivers for each operating system. This was a burden to hardware vendors (who created the drivers) and to any administrators who managed multiple operating systems.

The new Windows Driver Model (WDM) allows Windows 2000 and Windows 98 systems to use the same drivers. This technology benefits hardware vendors because they no longer need to maintain two sets of drivers. It benefits users because it increases the compatibility of Microsoft's high-end operating systems. It also benefits administrators because they will no longer need to maintain separate drivers for their Windows 98 users and for their Windows servers.

WDM has other advantages, too. Microsoft has done the bulk of the work required for creating device drivers. Hardware vendors still need to write a small minidriver for their product, but the time required for programming is significantly less.

The WDM Kernel Streaming architecture improves the performance of real-time streaming media. Previous versions of Windows required streaming media applications to do the bulk of processing in user mode. Many of these functions have been moved to kernel mode, where they execute much faster. Applications must be specifically written to take advantage of the WDM Kernel Streaming, however, so legacy applications will not benefit.

The WDM Still Image Architecture provides operating system–level support for scanners and digital cameras. With this support included within Windows 2000, users will benefit by having a consistent, tightly integrated interface for scanning and photography equipment. Previous versions of Windows required the hardware developer to write software to integrate his or her equipment into the operating system.

Enterprise Memory Architecture (EMA)

Memory allocation can create bottlenecks for many large application servers. This is particularly true for massive database servers that must handle hundreds of gigabytes of data. One of the improvements in Windows 2000 Server is the Enterprise Memory Architecture (EMA), which allows up to 32 GB of memory to be addressed by servers with 64-bit processors. Most servers will never need this much RAM, but data warehouses can benefit because data can be manipulated faster in memory than on hard disks. Not all computer systems are ready to use the large memory model, but the Alpha and Pentium II Xeon chips are already compatible.

Applications must be specifically coded to use the VLM (Very Large Memory) APIs. Microsoft SQL Server is coded to use this, and other relational database services will no doubt be modified to use the new APIs. Most applications will *not* benefit simply from adding more than 4 GB of RAM.

Better Multiprocessor Capabilities

For servers that are bottlenecked by the processor speed, Windows 2000 Server features greatly improved multiprocessor support. While Windows NT has always supported having more than a single processor, this newest generation of server software will utilize multiple processors more efficiently. All multithreaded applications executing on multiprocessor systems will perform better; developers do not need to write special code to take advantage of the improved scalability.

Windows 2000 Server supports two processors simultaneously, and existing users of Windows NT 4.0 Server who upgrade to Windows 2000 Server will be allowed to use four processors. Windows 2000 Advanced Server supports four simultaneous processors, and existing users of Windows NT 4.0 Server Enterprise Edition who upgrade to Windows 2000 Advanced Server can continue to use eight processors. Windows 2000 Advanced Server doubles the maximum number of processors from what was previously available—16 processors can be used simultaneously. Hardware vendors can extend that even further to support 32-way concurrent processing.

For the first time in a Windows operating system, processes can be pinned to specific processors. Administrators can use the Task Manager to set the processor *affinity* of a process. This forces the process to use only that specific processor, which can improve performance by reducing the number of processor cache flushes as processes are swapped between processors. Use this feature with caution, because it can also reduce performance by not allowing the process to move to the least busy processor.

I2O Support

I2O (Intelligent I/O Architecture) is a new technology that reduces the load on a system's CPU and improves I/O performance. I2O works by adding a dedicated processor that is optimized for input and output operations. This technology promises to streamline bandwidth-intensive activities such as real-time audio and video.

Improved Sorting

Large-scale databases and warehousing applications will realize performance improvements by using the improved sorting capabilities of Windows 2000 Advanced Server. Performance is greatly improved by moving these processor-intensive algorithms to the kernel. Applications will need to be written specifically to take advantage of the new APIs, and the newest version of Microsoft SQL Server already has been.

Changes to Support the Zero Administration for Windows Initiative

The Zero Administration for Windows initiative is covered in more detail in Chapter 3, but the architectural changes will be introduced here. Plug and Play is now supported, so administrators will spend less time configuring and troubleshooting hardware. Advanced Configuration and Power Interface (ACPI) improves the power efficiency of all Windows 2000 systems, reducing costs by directly reducing electrical requirements. Disk quotas will help administrators conserve drive space, reducing the need to purchase additional hardware. Remote boot functionality will allow desktop systems to be installed at a much faster pace than was previously possible.

Plug and Play

One of the most difficult aspects of managing computer networks is handling hardware configuration. In the past, configuring hardware required a detailed understanding of interrupts, I/O ports, and Direct Memory Access (DMA). Plug and Play technology has helped simplify the process of configuring hardware, but it has not been completely supported by all operating systems. Windows 95 and Windows 98 offer complete support of the protocol, but Windows NT 4.0 included only minimal support.

Windows 2000 Server has a more powerful Device Manager and Hardware Wizard than any previous version of Windows. These tools will more reliably detect and resolve hardware conflicts, decreasing administration time. This can mean more uptime for servers because administrators won't need to spend as long tweaking hardware configuration when adding new network cards, modems, or hard drives. The Device Manager is pictured in Figure 1-3 on the following page.

When the operating system boots, it will automatically detect new hardware and will launch the Hardware Wizard when an administrator logs in. Conflicts can often be detected and resolved automatically, and online help files are quickly available for those circumstances when the administrator must troubleshoot the hardware manually.

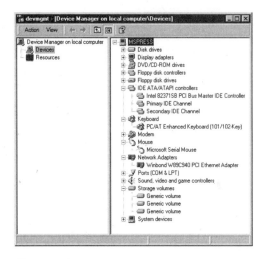

Figure 1-3.
*The Device Manager helps administrators configure and troubleshoot
hardware.*

OnNow/ACPI

The OnNow/ACPI initiative allows for greater control over how systems use
power. Laptop users will benefit more than anyone else; typically, administrators are not concerned about how much power a server uses. Regardless, the
new standards are implemented as part of the Windows Driver Model. Therefore, they are supported by Windows 2000 Server, as well as all other members
of the Windows 2000 family and Windows 98.

Disk Quotas

A new version of the NTFS file system is being introduced with the new version of Windows. One of the most interesting features is the ability to limit the
disk space consumed by users on specific partitions. This will allow administrators of file servers and web servers to tightly control how their users store files.
It is even possible to configure your drive so that it is impossible for users to
fill the partition!

Remote Boot

The new remote boot functionality included with Windows 2000 Server makes
it easier to control when desktop systems are powered on. While servers are
generally allowed to be powered on continuously, it is beneficial to shut down
user systems after-hours when they are not in use. Controlling when systems

boot from a central server also makes it simpler to configure large numbers of desktop systems, because they can be booted and configured without visiting each station.

Changes to support remote booting must, of course, be implemented within network cards and network card drivers. New network cards must be able to listen for boot requests even when the system is powered down. Microsoft has contributed to making this functionality standardized and has included support for it in the operating system. For more information on remote booting, please refer to Chapter 3, "Zero Administration for Windows."

Clustering

Organizations that depend on their networks require extremely high uptime. Downtime is one of the greatest contributors to a high total cost of ownership (TCO). Downtime is caused by several different events:

- Hardware failures
- Application failures
- Reboots as a result of configuration changes
- Upgrades and patches

The new clustering features of Windows 2000 Datacenter Server allow two servers to back each other up. Now, when one server fails, a second server can automatically take over those services in less than a minute, in a process known as *fail-over*. The monitoring services will detect the failure and shift responsibility to the backup server.

For scheduled downtime events, one server can cover for the other server while it is taken offline. This process, called a *rolling upgrade*, reduces downtime to a minimum when applying patches. Administrators benefit the most because they don't have to wait until after-hours to do upgrades! The results are extremely reliable network services and lower total cost of ownership.

One of the goals of clustering is to allow better scalability by load-balancing requests between multiple machines. While the focus of Microsoft's clustering efforts is to improve uptime by providing fail-over capabilities, many aspects of the operating system are capable of being load balanced. For example, file and printer shares can now be mirrored between multiple systems. Requests can be automatically distributed between two or more systems, and clients will automatically select a different server in the event one server in a cluster fails.

Clustering services are built into the operating system itself. This makes it easier for third-party software developers to use the Component Object Model (COM) to implement their own high-availability solutions. Clusters will be easy to manage because cluster-aware administration tools can change settings to multiple servers simultaneously. Unlike many third-party solutions, Windows 2000 Server does not require expensive or nonstandard hardware. You can take advantage of all the Windows 2000 Server clustering capabilities without purchasing any special equipment. Servers in the same cluster can even have different hardware configurations, allowing you to save money by purchasing a less expensive system as the backup server.

Several standard components have been improved to support fail-over between systems in a cluster:

- WINS (Windows Internet Name Service)
- DHCP (Dynamic Host Configuration Protocol)
- Dfs (Distributed File System)

More information on these distributed services is included in other chapters of this book.

Terminal Services

Windows 2000 Server is the first Windows operating system to ship with Terminal Services built in. These services allow clients to run interactive applications on a remote server. The client system merely accepts input from and displays output to the user. The network infrastructure is used to carry the data between the client system and the server. All processing is done on the server itself. This is illustrated in Figure 1-4. For Windows 2000 Server, this technology is often called Hydra, after the project name used while it was in development.

This new feature allows the use of thin clients and helps reduce the total cost of ownership of a network. A *thin client* is a desktop system that has a bare minimum of hardware. Instead of requiring end-user systems to have fast processors, large amounts of RAM, and large hard drives, the network Terminal Services will do all the work. The thin client will simply forward requests to the server. The experience for the user is similar to that of having a fully equipped desktop system. While hardware requirements for the client are minimal, Terminal Services may be used with any type of desktop system.

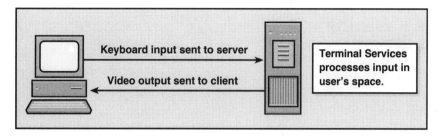

Figure 1-4.
Terminal Services takes a load off client systems by shifting application processing to the server.

CAN USE
OLD O/S PCS

The light requirements of the clients provide an added benefit to organizations with legacy hardware. Existing Windows for Workgroups 3.11 and Windows 95 systems can act as clients without upgrading the operating system. This allows an older piece of desktop hardware to run new 32-bit applications, increasing its lifetime. Of course, Terminal Services clients for Windows NT 4.0, Windows 95, Windows 98, and Windows 2000 Professional are also included with Windows 2000 Server.

Naturally, because the server is taking more of the total processing load off of the clients on the network, Terminal Services will require hardware that is more powerful. However, the additional cost is offset by the reduced client requirements. There are other cost-reducing benefits to this architecture. Applications are stored on the servers themselves, so administrators have fewer machines to update when changes are needed. Administrators also have greater control over the user environment because it is stored completely on the server.

Several aspects of the design of the Windows 2000 kernel were made to accommodate Terminal Services. Traditionally, Windows operating systems allowed a single interactive session, a session for a user who was sitting directly at the console and had physical access to the machine. To allow multiple users to each have a session over the network, Windows 2000 incorporates a highly modified Win32 subsystem. The new Win32 subsystem can track different user sessions and keep them separate. Keyboard and mouse input are funneled not only to the proper application, but also to the proper session. Each user does work within his or her own security limitations. These differences are illustrated in Figure 1-5 on the following page.

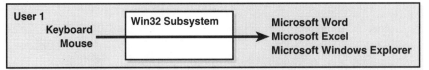

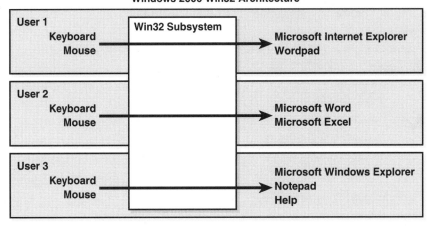

Figure 1-5.
The Windows 2000 Win32 subsystem is capable of handling multiple user sessions.

This is the most logical way to think of the new architecture. Technically, a separate Win32 process is launched for each user session. This ensures that applications do not communicate between user sessions, eliminating potential violations of a user's privacy. These kernel changes will not affect administrators who choose not to use Terminal Services. However, these changes are important to understand if you are planning to take advantage of them.

Globalization

The original Microsoft operating systems were intended for a United States audience. They provided only the Roman alphabet and English text, and did nothing to help developers write applications for other languages and cultures. The need for Windows was worldwide, however, and developers began to write applications for other countries. This development was difficult because the operating system was not specifically created with globalization in mind. As Windows has evolved, each generation has added more features to help users in other countries and the developers creating applications for those users. The Windows 2000 operating system has the most extensive set of globalization features of any Windows operating system.

The Windows 2000 kernel was designed specifically to support globalization. Unicode is used for every internal aspect, making it much simpler to adapt the operating system to multiple languages. NLS, the Native Language Support, allows location and language information to be stored in the registry and provides a uniform localization interface for applications to query. These features help developers create applications that will work in a variety of locales, and they help users customize their environment to their needs.

Unicode

Unicode refers to a standard created by the Unicode Consortium, an organization dedicated to creating standards that allow systems all over the world to communicate. The standard defines what bytes will correspond to which characters, similar to the ANSI standards. It is an improvement over ANSI, however, because a single character set is used for all languages. ANSI required a different character set for each language that needed a distinct alphabet.

> **N O T E :**   For more information on the Unicode Consortium, visit their Web site at *http://www.unicode.org.*

Unicode allows for many more characters than ANSI. ANSI uses 8-bit characters, so 256 characters can be supported—not nearly enough for uppercase and lowercase character sets in many languages. Unicode uses 16 bits for each character, providing up to 65,536 possibilities. Currently, 38,887 characters have been coded, covering the principal written languages of Africa, India, Asia, Europe, the Middle East, North America, and South America.

Unicode Fonts?

Unicode supports almost 40,000 characters. However, there is no font that can display all of these. Various fonts support various parts of the total Unicode character set, so different languages still require locale-specific fonts to be installed and used.

Windows 2000 supports Unicode and relies on it for everything internal to the operating system. For example, all NTFS file names are composed of Unicode characters. This allows the same file system to be used regardless of the locale in use on the operating system. Applications can be written to take advantage of Unicode, but not all applications need do so.

Native Language Support (NLS)

Native Language Support (NLS) allows administrators to configure an operating system with locale-specific information. The API has been part of Windows NT since the first version. It stores about one hundred settings in the registry and provides an interface to that information, allowing applications to easily determine what locale-specific settings should be used on a particular system.

Locale-specific information goes beyond remembering which language the user prefers. Different countries use different formats for dates, times, days of the week, money, and more. By providing a standard set of APIs, users do not need to configure individual applications for their environment. The operating system is configured once, and all applications can query the operating system's settings.

Only files required for the specific language and country are installed. The space consumed by these files is small compared to the space that would be required to install language support for all of the countries supported by Windows 2000.

Summary

The core of Windows 2000 Server is the kernel. The kernel is based on the same basic architecture as Windows NT Advanced Server 3.1 but has evolved to meet the changing needs of modern networks. The kernel now allows the operating system to scale higher, supporting up to 32 processors and 32 GB of RAM. It allows database applications like Microsoft SQL Server to take advantage of that larger hardware, and increases their performance by moving pieces of functionality into the kernel itself. Features such as processor quotas and process accounting make Windows 2000 Server an extremely attractive platform for web hosting environments. Clustering features are now built into the kernel, allowing for greatly improved uptime in networks where redundancy is available. Finally, Windows 2000 Server has the best support yet in a Windows operating system for globalization and localization, featuring flexible language and locale capabilities.

CHAPTER TWO

File Systems and Storage Management

The Windows 2000 File System

The NTFS file system was designed to allow for expandability. Microsoft Windows 2000 Server takes advantage of this design by offering many new features in NTFS 5 that use the same underlying NTFS format. Improved volume management allows administrators to expand and manage dynamic volumes without a reboot. Disk quotas keep user files within specified space guidelines. The Encrypting File System (EFS) reduces the chance that a malicious hacker can gain access to private files. Native disk defragmentation capabilities now include the defragmentation of NTFS volumes. Finally, the Distributed Link Tracking service ensures that when administrators move files around on a network, end users will still be able to locate them.

Volume Management

Dynamic volumes are a new concept, introduced with Windows 2000. They provide the same functionality as partitions but can be configured without the burden of rebooting the system. Windows 2000 will continue to support partitions and logical drives on legacy volumes, but administrators should upgrade to dynamic volumes on systems where backward compatibility is not necessary.

Volumes, unlike partitions, are not limited to four per hard drive. Additionally, administrators can now create, extend, and mirror volumes without rebooting the server. This allows server capacity to grow without interrupting users working on the server. Further, disk administration can now be done over the network; previous versions of Windows required administrators to be at the console of the system.

Microsoft considers partitions created by Microsoft Windows NT 4.0 or earlier to be *basic storage*. Windows 2000 Server supports basic storage for legacy reasons, but legacy volumes cannot be extended, and stripe sets and mirrors cannot be created. Basic storage can be upgraded to the new format, *dynamic storage,* at any time. Disks can be managed using the Computer Management MMC (Microsoft Management Console) snap-in. The snap-in provides a powerful suite of disk management tools, which administrators can use to

- Add new disks

- Create new volumes

- Mark partitions as active

- Add, delete, and extend volumes

- Create and destroy stripe sets

- Create, destroy, and repair RAID 1 and RAID 5 arrays

- Change basic storage partitions to dynamic storage volumes, and vice versa

The snap-in provides a friendly, wizard-oriented user interface. Figure 2-1 illustrates the new interface.

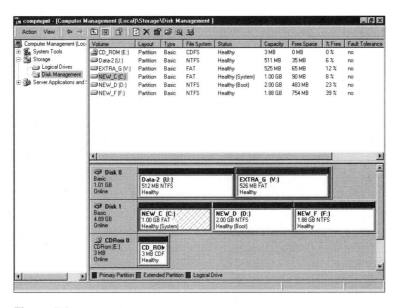

Figure 2-1.
The Computer Management snap-in allows the administration of disks.

Administrators who are upgrading their systems should be aware of a few changes. High Performance File System (HPFS) partitions, used for compatibility with OS/2, are no longer supported; they must be converted to NTFS before upgrading to Windows 2000 Server. Dynamic volumes have many advantages, but MS-DOS and any older version of Windows cannot view them—even if the administrator formatted them with the FAT file system.

Disk Quotas

One of the most common complaints about Windows from former UNIX administrators is the lack of a quota system to monitor and limit disk space consumed by users. In response to these complaints, Microsoft has included disk quotas as a native part of the Windows 2000 Server operating system. Disk quotas allow system administrators to specify the maximum amount of disk space any given user can consume. This ensures that no single user on a shared file system can use more than his or her share of space. It also means that administrators can now accurately predict disk space requirements and guarantee users of a network file server a certain amount of space. Combined with the process accounting described in Chapter 1, Internet Service Providers (ISPs) can reliably host hundreds of users on a single Web server.

Administrators can assign quotas on a group basis or on an individual user basis. Administrators configure two distinct values: the quota threshold and the quota limit. Once the user reaches the quota threshold, the server adds an event to the Event Log. Administrators should watch for these events and notify users when they have reached this warning level. When the disk space consumed by a user reaches the quota limit, that user will no longer be able to create new files until he or she clears up some disk space.

Some administrators have users who cannot tolerate the potential for lost work because of a full disk quota. If this is the case for you, set only the warning level quota threshold. This will send an alert to notify you that the user is consuming too much space, but it will never block the user from creating more files. Remember that you must configure quotas on a per-volume basis. Therefore, even if a user stores files outside of his or her home directory, the space those files consume still counts against the user's quota limit. File ownership is used to track which user account to charge disk space against. The space the file occupies is counted against a user's quota when he or she takes ownership of the file. For this reason, administrators and power users who might be taking ownership of other users' files should not have quotas enforced.

You can use Microsoft Windows Explorer to manage quotas. Simply view the properties for a root drive and click the Quota tab to control how the system enforces quotas on that volume. Figure 2-2 shows this interface. Clicking the Quota Entries button allows you to configure thresholds for individual users and groups.

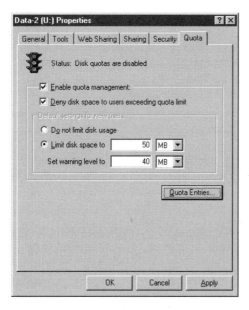

Figure 2-2.
Enable disk quotas using Windows Explorer.

The Encrypting File System (EFS)

Windows 2000 Server also adds encryption capabilities to NTFS. The Encrypting File System (EFS) uses a combination of encryption schemes, including public-key encryption and Data Encryption Standard (DES), to eliminate the possibility that someone could bypass file permissions and gain access to confidential data on your system. When you enable EFS for a file or folder on an NTFS volume, the operating system encrypts the files using the public-key algorithms available through the CryptoAPI. Though the underlying mechanism is complicated, administrators and end users can take advantage of the heightened security by merely selecting a check box in the Advanced Attributes dialog box, shown in Figure 2-3. This dialog box can be accessed by clicking the Advanced button on the File Properties dialog box.

Figure 2-3.
Enabling file encryption is as easy as selecting a check box.

Without EFS turned on, a malicious attacker with physical access to a system could boot to another operating system and gain access to files that have been secured with file permissions only. Risk is limited for physically secured servers, but mobile users will benefit from EFS in the event a laptop computer is stolen. Windows 2000 Server implements EFS as an integrated system service. It performs well enough that there is no noticeable speed difference when accessing encrypted files.

With EFS, each file is encrypted using both a randomly generated key and the user's private key. The fact that the files are encrypted means they will be unrecognizable to other operating systems. Further, using a randomly generated key reduces the chances that a cryptoanalysis-based attack can be used to decode the file. Only a user with the private key can decrypt the files. A recovery key is created during the encryption process for administrators who need to recover files—for example, when an employee leaves a company.

Please note that EFS is strictly for security of stored information; data stored in remote EFS-protected files is not encrypted when traversing the network. This first release of EFS relies on DES. For more information on the cryptography features of Windows 2000 Server, please refer to Chapter 5.

Disk Defragmentation

Files are often divided into several pieces when they are written to a hard drive. Files that are divided into more than one segment on a disk are *fragmented*. This is perfectly normal and does not affect a user's ability to access the file. However, performance is faster if the file is stored in one contiguous section. Over time, fragmentation can have a severe impact on the performance of a server. This is particularly true of busy file servers and web servers where updates happen frequently.

Previous versions of Windows included the ability to defragment FAT file systems. Third-party products were available to defragment NTFS drives, but Windows NT 4 included no such software. The only options available to administrators who needed to defragment an NTFS partition were to purchase additional software or reformat the partition.

Windows 2000 Server now includes the native capability to defragment any type of writable volume: FAT, FAT32, and NTFS. The included defragmentation software was originally created by Executive Software. The version that ships with the operating system is somewhat limited—administrators can initiate defragmentation only manually and only on the local system. However, defragmentation can occur online without interrupting service to the particular volume.

Defragmentation is controlled through the Disk Defragmenter MMC snap-in. It can be easily accessed by viewing the properties of a drive, selecting the Tools tab, and clicking the Defragment button. The snap-in, as shown in Figure 2-4, provides a simple interface to drive defragmentation.

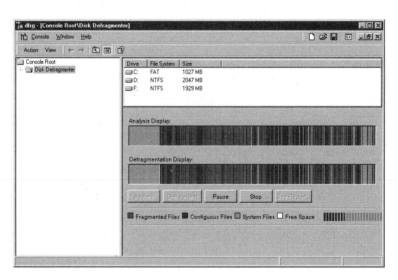

Figure 2-4.
Windows 2000 Server includes an NTFS defragmentation utility.

Distributed Link Tracking

Distributed Link Tracking helps users find the destination for a shortcut when the file has moved. It is also used to locate OLE links when the destination object is not where it is expected to be. Files created in Windows 2000 on NTFS volumes use two separate IDs to identify the file and its location: the *birth* location and the *revised* location. When a file is created, both the birth and revised locations are set to indicate the system and volume on which the file is created. However, if that file is later moved to another volume or another system entirely, the birth location stays the same and only the revised location changes. The birth location, therefore, never changes during the life of a file.

If a user accesses a shortcut and the destination file cannot be found, the link-tracking service on the local machine will begin a search for the destination file. This search can span other volumes on the system which formerly hosted the file, as well as a master list of birth and revised locations that resides on domain controllers. In most cases, the file can be identified and the shortcut destination can be updated. To allow for tracking of files and volumes moved between servers in the same domain, domain controllers have a Link Tracking Server service that provides an interface to a database replicated throughout the domain. This database tracks associations between birth and revised locations.

Distributed Link Tracking improves upon a problem with older versions of Windows—broken shortcuts. Previous versions of Windows allowed users to search the local system for the shortcut destination, but files and applications located on remote servers could not be found. Now administrators can move files between volumes on a file server, move files between servers, move entire volumes between servers, rename servers, and change shares without leaving users stranded.

Miscellaneous Improvements

Windows 2000 includes several other noteworthy improvements to the file system. Security descriptors can be used once to reference multiple files, thereby saving disk space. Applications can create a special type of file called a *sparse file*. Sparse files allow an application to allocate a great deal of space but not actually consume that space—it will be allocated as the application actually writes data to the file. The CHKDSK utility, which is capable of checking and fixing errors on a volume, is much faster than in Windows NT 4.0. Finally, Windows 2000 supports the FAT32 file system for compatibility with Windows 98, in addition to the FAT and NTFS file systems.

Shared Folders

The clumsy interface of resource-related components in the Server Manager in Control Panel has been replaced by Shared Folders, an MMC snap-in, as illustrated in Figure 2-5 on the following page. The new Windows Explorer–like interface allows administrators to quickly create and manage shares on the local system or remote machines. Shared Folders can be used to manage any Windows 2000 or Windows NT 4.0 system. This utility is particularly useful when used with Microsoft Dfs (distributed file system) trees, because it allows the tree to be built and managed more easily than would otherwise be possible. Dfs is described in more detail in Chapter 9.

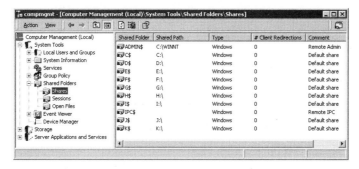

Figure 2-5.
*The new Shared Folders interface makes handling shares and share
permissions easier than ever.*

Shared Folders does more than just manage shares. It allows administrators and server operators to view which users are connected to which shares, to modify permissions associated with shares, and to view which files are being used. Administrators can also send a message to users of a particular resource; for example, to warn users before a particular network resource is removed.

A feature new to Windows 2000 is the caching of network documents for offline use. This is similar to the Briefcase features built in to Windows 95, Windows 98, and Windows NT 4.0, but it has been extended to the enterprise network. Caching documents allows a user with a laptop computer to create a local copy of network documents, modify those documents while not connected to the network, and resynchronize the documents when the network is again available. There are three different caching schemes: manual document caching, automatic document caching, and automatic program caching.

Manual document caching requires that users specify which files they want to be cached locally for offline use. Automatic document caching caches *all* files that are accessed over the network; the user need do nothing except use a network resource to make a cached copy of it available while offline. Automatic program caching is useful for network applications that store the executable on a remote share. Users who run the application can continue to do so even after they have disconnected from the network. Further, network traffic will be reduced because the local cached copy of the program will be used even if the user is connected to the network. This last option must be used only on read-only shares.

Removable Storage

Windows NT 4.0 had no native support for tape changers or jukeboxes. The burden of supporting this hardware was shifted to third-party software and hardware vendors. Windows 2000 Server supports these features for the first time in a Windows operating system, with Removable Storage. Removable Storage makes it easier to manage data that is stored across multiple tapes or CD-ROMs. It also labels, catalogs, and tracks all types of media. Removable Storage is capable of controlling tape changers and even handles automatic cleanings. Removable Storage is merely an interface to the media that backup software uses. It does not actually handle the backup or restoration of files—these services are provided by the backup software described in the next section.

Removable Storage tracks media by grouping it into libraries. There are three types of libraries available: online libraries, stand-alone libraries, and offline libraries. An online library is any device that holds multiple drives or tapes, such as a tape changer. Stand-alone libraries hold one piece of media at a time; Removable Storage must rely on an administrator to change the media when necessary. The offline library is used to track all media that is not currently accessible to Removable Storage. For example, if you ship tapes off-site, Removable Storage will move them into the offline library.

Removable Storage categorizes different types of media into media pools. For example, writable CDs and backup tapes would belong in separate media pools. These pools are further classified as either unrecognized, free, application, or import media pools. Media in the unrecognized media pool are new and can be moved to the free media pool, which tracks blank media that are ready to be used. Application media pools are created by backup applications to track used media. The import media pool contains media that have not been catalogued by Removable Storage; once catalogued, the media will be moved into either the free or application media pools.

Removable Storage has many features that enable it to scale to enterprise proportions. Security can be configured for different devices so that specific operators manage specific hardware. Requests for backups and restores are queued, prioritized, and managed using the snap-in interface, as shown in Figure 2-6 on the next page. This interface allows administrators to control Removable Storage from anywhere in the network. Finally, Removable Storage activities can be automated through the use of the command-line interface and batch files.

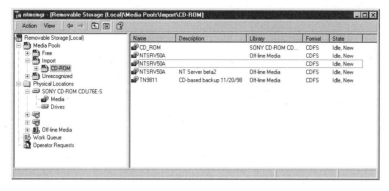

Figure 2-6.
Removable Storage helps administrators track different types of media.

Backup and Recovery

The backup and recovery software in Windows 2000 Server is a great improvement over previous generations of Windows. It has been provided by Seagate Software, which has a history of creating excellent backup software for Windows operating systems. The new utility includes backup and restore wizards and easier access to network resources. Additionally, more media types are supported, including hard disks, zip drives, writable CDs, and tape drives. Windows NT administrators often had to purchase third-party applications to meet their backup requirements. Now many environments will be able to perform enterprise backups with Windows 2000 Server right out of the box.

The new backup utility is *not* an MMC snap-in. It is accessible through the Accessories program group within the Start menu. As shown in Figure 2-7, it provides an easy-to-use, graphical user interface that allows administrators to initiate backups and restores, and schedule jobs to occur in the future. It includes standard features of backup software, such as full backups, differential backups, and incremental backups. It also allows for scheduled and batch-initiated backups. It relies on Removable Storage to manage backup media.

Another feature new to this most recent revision of the backup software is the Disaster Recovery Preparation Wizard. This wizard helps you prepare for a failure of the system by backing up system files *and* emergency repair information that might not otherwise be captured. Previous versions of Windows required that administrators use a special repair disk utility, which was cumbersome when backing up multiple servers.

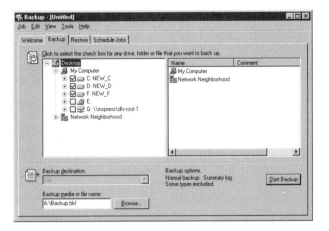

Figure 2-7.
The new backup utility is more robust than previous generations.

Hierarchical Storage Management (HSM)

Computer users think of disk drives as providing data storage for computer systems, tape drives as storing backup information, and CDs as providing long-term data storage. A feature new to Windows 2000 Server is Hierarchical Storage Management (HSM). HSM allows different types of media to be part of the same file system. Remote Storage will move unused files to less expensive forms of data storage automatically, when configured by an administrator to do so.

For example, Windows 2000 Server can move files located on an NTFS partition that have not been touched in two months onto a tape backup system. The next time the user attempts to retrieve the file, the server will automatically pull the file off tape. The user will be subject to a delay while the file is transferred, but it will be otherwise transparent. Files can also be moved when disk space begins to run low, allowing for an automatically expanding file system.

Remote Storage is administered using a dedicated MMC interface, a special tab on file and directory properties, and Disk Administrator. Remote Storage makes use of Removable Storage to provide an interface to different types of media. Third-party vendors can integrate their products into HSM by using a special application programming interface (API) provided by Microsoft.

Summary

Windows 2000 continues to improve on Microsoft operating systems by including stronger storage and backup capabilities. The cornerstone of these new features is NTFS 5, a new version of the partition format designed specifically for Windows. Dynamic volumes offer powerful online storage management functions but are not backward compatible with legacy operating systems. You can now create and delete partitions, volumes, and RAID arrays. Disk quotas can help eliminate disk space shortages on file servers because you can restrict the amount of disk space each user or group consumes.

Data security is also increased. The Encrypting File System (EFS) greatly reduces the chance that a malicious hacker will gain access to secure data, while not limiting an administrator's ability to access the data in an emergency.

For the first time, disk defragmentation can be performed on NTFS volumes, as well as on FAT and FAT32 partitions. Previously the only way to improve performance on a fragmented disk was reformatting. Users will never misplace a file again, thanks to the Link Tracking Server service, which maintains a database of files and their current locations. This database is used by client systems to locate files that have been moved since they were last accessed. The new Shared Folders MMC snap-in offers a powerful user interface that enables administrators to easily manage how resources are shared. This tool complements the distributed file system very well; you can create a Dfs tree consisting of shares throughout your enterprise with a single MMC console.

Removable Storage provides administrators with tools to manage tape changers, and provides software developers with a simple API for handling complex backup hardware. Now locating a critical backup tape will be quicker and easier than ever before. In addition, the native backup utility is improved from Windows NT 4.0. It now allows you to utilize different types of media, such as writable CDs. Further, backups are easier because of a graphical scheduling utility and a disaster recovery wizard. Another new feature of Windows 2000 Server is Hierarchical Storage Management (HSM), which enables the transparent transfer of seldom-used files to cheaper media formats. Volumes can be almost limitless in size because rarely used files can be moved to less expensive tape media. The new Windows 2000 Server file system has been designed to meet the high-end requirements of enterprise networks while keeping costs at a minimum.

PART II

ZERO ADMINISTRATION FOR WINDOWS

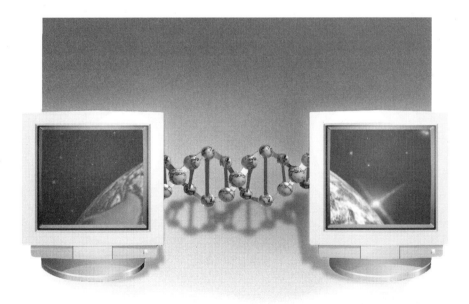

Zero Administration
for Windows

What Is TCO?

Computers and networks are used to save organizations money. Almost without argument, it is more efficient for an accounting department to use a network of computers than to use simpler tools such as calculators and pencils. Computers provide a powerful and flexible tool for users. Networks link these tools and encourage the sharing of information.

Though computers do save companies money, they also cost a lot of money. It becomes increasingly important to reduce the total cost of ownership (TCO) associated with computers as networks grow in size. However, calculating the actual costs of computer networks is more complicated than it might seem.

The most thorough research into this topic was performed by the Gartner Group. As shown in Figure 3-1 on the next page, 12 percent of the TCO was attributed to administration costs. Sixteen percent was caused each by technical support and hardware and software purchases. The majority of the total cost, a surprising 56 percent, was attributed to lost productivity by end users.

Users lose productivity for several reasons. If a server fails, they might not be able to access critical files or execute network applications. If the network fails, they not only lose access to their servers but to every network resource. Users also lose productivity spending time learning the operating system and various applications on the operating system. In some environments, users *wasted* time with unproductive applications that had not been approved by the administrators.

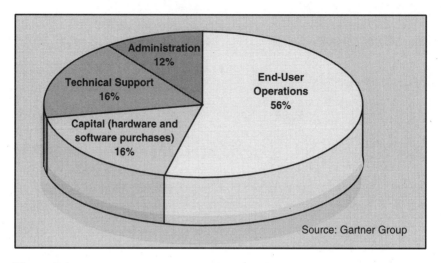

Figure 3-1.
The most costly part of computer networks is attributable to end-user lost productivity.

Why Zero Administration for Windows?

The Zero Administration for Windows initiative attempts to reduce TCO by directly addressing the issues that cost organizations the most money. As described in this chapter, networks based on Microsoft Windows 2000 Server will benefit in many ways:

- Users can move between systems and keep all the same desktop settings *and* applications.

- New systems can be installed with minimal administrative effort.

- Existing systems can be updated and upgraded quickly.

- Applications can be updated in a central location and pushed out to client systems as they are needed.

- The desktop environment can be locked down to minimize the amount of unapproved changes a user makes to the operating system.

- User data can be mirrored between the desktop system and the server, allowing for quick restores when a failure occurs.

- Data located on network servers can be cached on user machines, allowing the user to continue work while offline.

IntelliMirror

Networks have become a critical part of the computing environment. We have become so dependent on the network that a failure often results in work stoppage for the users. For example, users whose profiles are stored on the network might not be able to log on to their system if the server fails. Even if they can log on, they might be missing their normal settings. It is common practice for users to store their files on the file server—but if they cannot connect to it, they cannot do any work.

IntelliMirror is designed to solve these problems. The IntelliMirror technologies will ensure that users can be productive even when they cannot connect to the server. This will reduce the enormous cost experienced when a network outage occurs, because users can continue working—often without realizing that a failure occurred.

This is accomplished by mirroring data between clients and servers. It happens in both directions—data that is normally stored on the client, such as desktop preferences, are mirrored to the server. Data kept permanently on the server, such as centralized documents, are mirrored to clients when they are accessed. This way, if a user switches computers, his or her desktop preferences can be copied from the server. If a user loses access to the server, he or she can continue to work on a cached copy of a document residing on that server. After the user reconnects, the server copy will be synchronized with his or her updates to the cached copy.

These technologies are not new. Rather, they are evolving. Roaming profiles were available with Windows 95 and Windows NT, allowing a user to move from one desktop system to another while maintaining a consistent set of desktop preferences. Windows 2000 Server improves on this by allowing entire applications—not just settings—to follow the user.

Windows 95 introduced the Briefcase, a metaphor for a simple utility that allowed copying and synchronization of files among computers on a network. It was intended to help users keep a single document current when they switched between a desktop and a laptop. Windows 2000 improves this concept by providing greater automation, transparently caching files for the end user and updating them when possible.

The IntelliMirror technologies each operate independently. Administrators are not compelled to centralize desktop settings on a server simply because they want to take advantage of client-side caching. Choose which features will benefit your environment the most, and use those to reduce the total cost of ownership for your organization.

Client-Side Caching

One of the most useful aspects of IntelliMirror is client-side caching of networked documents and applications. Using this technology, end users can access files located on a network server *even when not attached to the network*. Administrators have the capability to specify which IntelliMirror shares can be cached, and can even choose from three different levels of caching. This is done at the time the share is created by clicking Caching on the Sharing tab from the Properties dialog box to bring up the Caching Settings dialog box, shown in Figure 3-2.

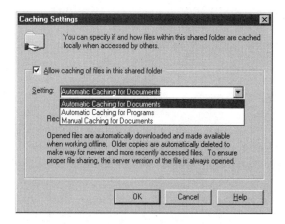

Figure 3-2.
Administrators control the type of caching clients will do for a particular share.

The Automatic Caching For Documents option directs the client system to create a local copy of all files accessed within that share. The client will always attempt to read the file from the server, but will use the local copy if the server is not available. This ensures that the user is always viewing the most up-to-date version of the document available.

The Automatic Caching For Programs option is used for read-only shares. Clients will download the data and will *not* refer to the network share each time the file is accessed. The name is somewhat deceiving—though it works well for applications that seldom modify files, you might also select this for shares containing rarely updated documents associated with any kind of application.

Selecting Manual Caching For Documents gives users the option of caching files in that share. The user must use Windows Explorer to specify that his or her computer should keep a copy of the files locally, as shown in Figure 3-3. If the user does not take these manual steps, the files will not be available when the user is offline.

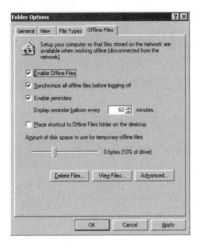

Figure 3-3.
Users can control which shares and which files their system should keep cached locally.

Files the user specifies are cached on the client system and accessed from the local hard drive when the system is detached from the network. This process is entirely transparent to the user—he or she accesses the file using the network drive connection just as if he or she were connected. The operating system redirects the user to the locally cached copy of the document.

For the first time, a user can edit a file on a network server at the office, and then take his or her laptop on the road and continue editing the file. The user can use the Synchronization Manager to update the server when the laptop is reconnected to the network. Synchronization Manager is an application that can be launched from the Accessories group of the Programs menu.

Administrators and users can also *pin* files to ensure that they remain in the client's cache. Files that are not pinned will be removed from the cache when the client runs low on disk space. Users can configure their own disk space thresholds using the Windows Explorer interface.

Remote Installation Service

Administrators can now power on and boot desktop systems without an operating system installed. This is similar to booting a system with a floppy disk that connects to a network server to launch a setup routine, but it is more sophisticated. Computers with a special PXE (Pre-Boot eXecution) boot ROM do not require a floppy disk at all, allowing floppyless workstations to be installed from the network.

To use Remote Installation Service (RIS), you must have several components on your network, but these components do not necessarily need to be running on separate systems. Indeed, all of this software can run on a single server:

- **DHCP Servers**   DHCP Servers provide the client an IP address as it starts to boot.

- **DNS Servers**   DNS is used to locate the Active Directory servers on the network.

- **Active Directory Servers**   Active Directory servers contain the information about RIS on the network.

- **RIS Servers**   RIS servers actually store the information about the operating system required for the client to boot.

Installing with a Floppy Disk

The RIS boot floppy is compatible with most common network cards, but not with all of them. The Network Interface Cards (NICs) you can use are

- 3Com 3C900, 3C900B, 3C905, 3C905B

- AMD PC Net and PC Fast Net

- HP DeskDirect 10/100 TX

- Intel Pro 10+, Pro 100+, Pro 100B, and E100B Series

- SMC 8432, 9332, and 9432

- Compaq NetFlex II and NetFlex III

Whether the system is booted from a floppy disk or the boot ROM, it will query the network to find a DHCP server that has BINL (Boot Information Negotiation Layer) extensions enabled. This network server, typically a Windows 2000 Server, will provide an IP address to the client. If the administrator has *prestaged* the system, BINL will create an object for the system within Active Directory. BINL will then direct the client to a Remote Installation server that has a bootable image of an operating system ready for the client to download.

The RIS system will query Active Directory to determine what boot image should be passed to the client. The setup files are transferred using the Trivial File Transfer Protocol (TFTP). TFTP is an old, UDP-based Internet standard used to quickly transfer small files. Typically, the first few files transferred to the client will be NTLdr, OSChooser, and SetupLdr.

The file server can provide a setup routine for the operating system, allowing quick provisioning of network clients. The remote booting capability can also be used for thin clients that have minimal hard drive space. The thin client does not need to store a local copy of the operating system; instead, the operating system is stored on an IntelliMirror server. The server will store a unique copy of the operating system for each client on the network. This allows for complete customization, overcoming a weakness in other models. To improve the efficiency of the storage, the Single Instance Store (SIS) model is used.

Single Instance Store

Single Instance Store is a technology developed to reduce disk space used when duplicate files are stored on a system. SIS can actually reduce the disk space consumed by multiple copies of operating systems for remote boot by 90 percent! IntelliMirror makes it easy for administrators to use SIS—there is no user interface. IntelliMirror handles everything automatically.

SIS works by replacing duplicate copies of files with links to a single, master copy of the file. A groveler agent scans the RIS volume on a regular basis and links redundant files. These links are tracked so that they can be updated when the original file is moved. Every time the administrator adds additional Remote Installation Preparation images to the RIS server, the agent will automatically scan the files and clean up wasted space.

Remote Installation Service Setup Wizard

Remote installations require the operating system source files to reside on an IntelliMirror server. The same files are located on the Windows 2000 Professional CD-ROM. The server must have copies of those files to send to clients, as well as configuration information set according to the administrator's preferences.

This distribution point is simple to create because it is driven by a wizard interface, as illustrated in Figure 3-4. This is an improvement over previous versions of Windows NT that required the administrator to complete many manual steps to create a distribution point for an operating system.

Figure 3-4.
Creating a distribution point for Windows 2000 Professional is entirely wizard-driven.

The wizard will prompt the administrator for a description of the distribution, as shown in Figure 3-5. This description will be read by the person who performs the setup using the Client Installation Wizard, so it should be detailed enough to allow the user to choose the correct distribution. After all the information has been provided, the wizard will prompt the administrator to insert the Windows 2000 Professional CD. The necessary setup files are copied from the CD and placed onto the IntelliMirror distribution point. (This can be a long process because several hundred megabytes must be transferred.)

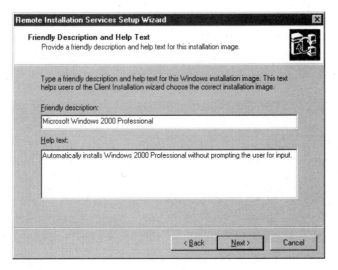

Figure 3-5.
Enter a description that will help people choose the correct distribution point.

Managing the Distribution Point

After the Remote Installation Service Setup Wizard has finished creating a distribution point, it can be managed using Active Directory Users and Computers, as shown in Figure 3-6. The RIS information is stored within Active Directory as an object and inherits all the benefits thereof. Administrators can restrict and delegate access to the properties of the distribution, allowing it to be managed by specific people within the organization.

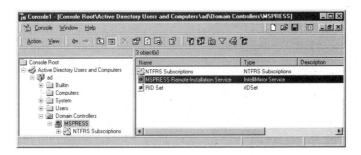

Figure 3-6.
RIS distributions are handled as an object within Active Directory Users and Computers.

Several properties of the distribution point can be modified with Active Directory Users and Computers. By default, computers are named based on the name of the user initiating the setup. This can be altered, as illustrated in Figure 3-7. You can also manage the list of installation choices and change their descriptions. Maintenance and troubleshooting tools can also be specified. These tools can be called on by users or administrators if the setup does not succeed.

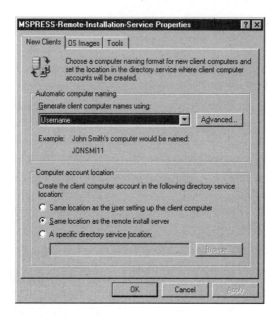

Figure 3-7.
By default, the computer name is based on the user's name.

Client Installation Wizard

Some input from the user might be desirable as the client system begins the installation process using the remote installation server. The process of querying the user for different pieces of information is accomplished with the Client Installation Wizard. This wizard is a trimmed-down version of the standard Windows 2000 setup routine, and can be configured by the administrator to guide the end user through the process as easily as possible.

The administrator has control over which options users are presented with. The Group Policy snap-in can allow help desk staff full control over the installation settings but provide standard users with only a minimum number of choices. The Client Installation Wizard can take four different paths: Automatic Setup, Custom Setup, Restart A Previous Setup Attempt, and Maintenance And Troubleshooting.

Automatic Setup Option

By default, any user can access the Automatic Setup option. This choice results in the minimal amount of user interaction. The operating system is set up entirely hands-free based on information provided by the administrators at the remote installation server. This is the ideal choice if it fits into your organization's structure because it reduces the chances that the user will need to place a support call.

RIS administrators have the ability to create multiple templates for automatic setup and provide the user with a choice. For example, it might be beneficial to have a separate setup route for the accounting, marketing, and management groups. Each of these groups uses a different suite of applications, and the user would not have any problem choosing which group he or she belonged in.

For best results, limit the number of choices presented to the user to five or less. Provide as detailed a description as necessary for each option, and be sure all users will be capable of determining which installation option is right for them. The goal of automatic setup is to reduce the burden of operating system installations; making it simple for the users will reduce the amount of effort required from the information systems staff.

Custom Setup Option

The Custom Setup option within the Client Installation Wizard functions similarly to the Automatic Setup option but includes greater flexibility. This choice is intended for cases where information systems staff will be standing in front of the machine while it boots. Among other things, it allows the administrator to specify the name and location of the computer within Active Directory—for cases where the automatically generated name is not sufficient.

This option should be used in all environments where the end user is not responsible for installing his or her own operating system. Because it requires an IT (information technology) staff member to be physically in front of the machine during setup, it increases the time and cost of provisioning. This option should also be used when systems have been prestaged by adding them into Active Directory before launching setup.

Restart a Previous Setup Attempt Option

If setup fails, it might be desirable to restart the previous attempt rather than begin a new installation. This will avoid asking the user the same questions again. For example, if you are using a custom setup that prompts for monitor resolution, network protocols, and company name, restarting the attempt will save the user from answering those questions again. Instead, the setup routine will read the previously entered answers from the text file they are stored in. It is best to direct users to contact information systems support in situations where an automatic setup routine has failed.

Maintenance And Troubleshooting Option

This option can be used to call programs that are outside the standard setup procedure. For example, if the administrator wants to run a BIOS update before installing the operating system, the BIOS update tool can be accessed from this menu option. This responsibility can even be delegated to the end user if the directions are straightforward. Like any other setup option, this choice can be restricted by changing the permissions on the installation setup answer file (SIF) for the tool.

Not all tools can be integrated into the RIS environment. They must be written specifically to be compatible with SIF. Contact your hardware vendor to determine whether they provide any such tools.

Group Policy Objects

Windows 2000 Server provides several built-in levels of security, such as Users, Power Users, and Administrators. These groups have been configured with specific rights that fit many organizations' needs. However, many organizations need a more granular permissions structure to allow some users more privileges than the default Users group allows, and others need to tighten security. To provide this granular control over permissions, administrators of Windows 2000 networks can use group policies.

Group policies are similar to the System Policy Editor included with Windows NT Server 4.0. That utility allowed administrators to enforce system-level and user-level restrictions, such as which icons appeared on the desktop, what applications users could run, and what screen saver could be used. Group policies perform these functions and go a step further.

Group Policy Snap-In

This utility is similar to the System Policy Editor, but it allows administrators greater control. Administrators can now use the Group Policy snap-in to create and apply a policy to any site, domain, or organizational unit. For example, an administrator could create policies such that users within the marketing.mspress.microsoft.com domain have the rights to change the screen resolution, but users within the accounting.mspress.microsoft.com domain do not.

Other aspects of a group's security can be changed as well. Password uniqueness, age, and length can be restricted. Access to the registry and file systems can be limited. Additionally, security surrounding the system services can be tightened. The Group Policy snap-in, as shown in Figure 3-8, is an MMC snap-in that must be added manually to the MMC interface.

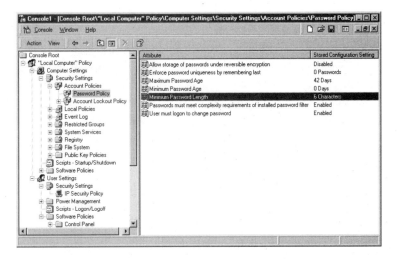

Figure 3-8.
The Group Policy snap-in replaces the System Policy Editor and adds functionality.

Software Policies

Software policies can be set to customize registry settings. These settings are manipulated to change the user's ability to modify system services, desktop settings, and application settings. Software policies can modify any part of the registry and can be used to configure third-party or custom applications. The Group Policy snap-in is also used to modify these software policies, as shown in Figure 3-9.

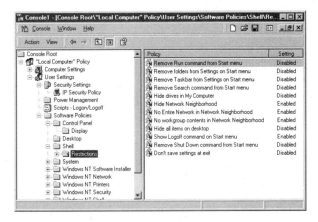

Figure 3-9.
The Group Policy snap-in allows administrators to restrict the user's ability to modify system services, desktop settings, and application settings.

Scripts

Windows 2000 Server can transfer a script to a client machine for execution at logon, logoff, startup, or shut down. These scripts are applied with the Group Policy snap-in, and can be applied to users, groups, or systems. Combined with the Windows Script Host, administrators have a powerful tool to perform automated tasks on user systems. Typical uses of logon and logoff scripts are to modify environment variables, mount or dismount file shares, and alert an administrator or manager of the user's actions.

Previous versions of Windows allowed logon scripts to be executed, but only a single script could be selected. Windows 2000 is the first to offer logoff scripts, and either logon or logoff scripts can be chosen using a simple graphical user interface, as illustrated in Figure 3-10.

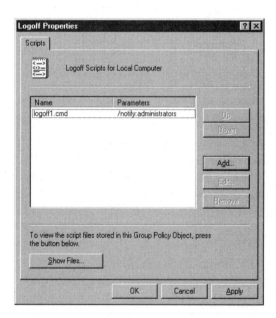

Figure 3-10.
The Group Policy snap-in allows administrators to specify logon and logoff scripts.

Application Management

Many administrators struggle to keep applications running. Applications can break for many different reasons—users fiddling with files, network applications being moved, and faulty upgrade routines cause many of the problems. Windows 2000's

TCO reduction initiative includes tighter administrative control over applications by using two new technologies—the Windows Installer and the Software Installation MMC snap-in.

Windows Installer

The Windows Installer is a transaction-based installation structure that applications use to place files and configuration settings on a system. It ensures that applications are installed in a standardized, controlled way. The Windows Installer tracks how files are copied to the system, and can accurately determine whether common files are still required when uninstalling an application. It also tracks Registry entries and shortcuts. The operating system can use this information to move, remove, and reinstall applications with a high level of control. Administrators can allow users to perform these actions, even if they do not have the proper file permissions—Windows Installer runs as a service and uses its own security context.

Rolling out patches and upgrades is now easier than ever. Just-in-time installations use the Windows Installer to add components to applications and apply patches when they are needed. The Windows Installer facilitates this by using Active Directory to locate the source files on the network, similar to the way Microsoft Internet Explorer can intelligently upgrade itself over the Internet.

You can take advantage of the Windows Installer even if you do not migrate your entire network to Windows 2000. Microsoft will provide service packs to add the service for Windows NT 4.0, Windows 95, and Windows 98.

The underlying mechanisms for this magic are Microsoft Installer (MSI) packages. An MSI package is a relational database filled with everything the operating system needs to know about installing the application. The package describes file locations, Registry settings, upgrade details, and repair information. New applications for Windows 2000 will be shipped with MSI packages, and administrators can create their own MSI packages for existing applications. MSI complements, but does not replace, Microsoft Systems Management Server (SMS). MSI cannot inventory hardware, schedule deployments, or create reports.

Software Installation MMC Snap-in

The Windows Installer is a service that manages application installations on Windows systems. Administrators must use the Software Installation snap-in to direct the service. Software Installation allows administrators to assign applications to specific users—making it simple to deploy applications in environments where users use multiple computers, or multiple users work on a single system.

Built-In Application Services

One of the most significant factors in TCO is custom development. Microsoft analyzed the type of work developers spend the most time doing and found a way to reduce the effort required to create a network application. Microsoft built services into Windows 2000 Server to provide interprocess and interserver communications through a simple interface that could be easily administered. These services are the Component Services (formerly Microsoft Transaction Services) and Message Queuing Services (formerly Microsoft Messaging Queue Services); both were introduced as part of the Internet Information Services (IIS) 4.0 Option Pack (available for Windows NT 4.0). The user interface, as illustrated in Figure 3-11, will look familiar to many because the first releases of Component Services were MMC snap-ins.

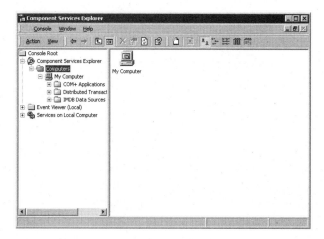

Figure 3-11.
The Component Services snap-in allows administrators to configure application objects.

With these services integrated into the operating system, developers can concentrate on business logic instead of network transport. Applications can be stored on a single system or distributed among multiple systems—without requiring any additional coding. The interfaces are beneficial to developers because they reduce the amount of code required to write a network application. They are also beneficial to administrators who have the freedom to change the architecture as the company's needs change.

Reduced Downtime

Downtime is a significant factor in the cost of computer networks. As such, reducing downtime has been one of the major goals for the upgrade of Windows NT 4.0 Server. Windows 2000 Server will require fewer reboots than any other Windows operating system. Some of the most common configuration changes that no longer require reboots are

- Changing IP addresses
- Adding and removing network protocols
- Changing audio and video drivers

As described in Chapter 1, the Plug and Play standards are part of Windows 2000 Server. This will reduce downtime by decreasing the number of hardware problems administrators experience. Though problems will undoubtedly still occur, improvements in Windows 2000 Server will minimize downtime. Online help files, for example, are readily available to walk the administrator through the process of troubleshooting the hardware.

Summary

The Zero Administration for Windows initiative is Microsoft's solution for reducing the total cost of ownership of computer networks. Technologies such as IntelliMirror reduce costs by improving the availability of network data. Remote Installation Services significantly decreases the time required to install, upgrade, and repair new desktop computers. Group policy objects allow administrators to restrict a user's work environment, keeping each system stable and the user productive. The new application management features ensure that network applications are always available and up-to-date.

CHAPTER FOUR

Other System Management Tools

Microsoft is on a mission to establish Windows 2000 Server as the preeminent enterprise platform. Efforts such as the Zero Administration for Windows initiative attract the most attention in this context, and the tools and technologies found under the Zero Administration for Windows umbrella will probably be the ones you'll become most familiar with. However, there are some other important capabilities incorporated into Windows 2000 that we'll take a look at in this chapter. The features we'll examine each play a role in the Zero Administration for Windows initiative but rarely make the headlines when Zero Administration for Windows is discussed. In fact, one of these features, the Windows Scripting Host (WSH), has had relatively little exposure to date but is likely to become one of the unsung heroes of Windows 2000 among system administrators.

The features we'll look at in this chapter are

- Windows Management Instrumentation (WMI)
- Windows Scripting Host (WSH)

Microsoft usually discusses these features under the heading of Microsoft Management Infrastructure. Indeed, they are both important infrastructure components that rely on other tools or applications to make use of the information they manage. Frequently, the Microsoft Management Console (MMC) is discussed in the same forum, although MMC is a much more visible tool within the system management context.

Briefly, here's a summary of the function of both of these features.

Function of Windows Management Instrumentation (WMI)

WMI relates specifically to device management. Microsoft's intention for WMI is that all the device drivers on a Windows system will support the WMI defined interfaces, thus providing a standardized means for the drivers to interact. WMI-enabled drivers will record items such as performance counters, error statistics, and device failure alerts that can be subsequently accessed by applications designed to report such information.

Function of Windows Scripting Host (WSH)

WSH is typically used to create administrative tools, but it has other capabilities as well. It represents the first architectural improvement for scripting since batch files were created for MS-DOS. WSH is not, itself, a language. Instead, it is a framework that allows any language interpreter to be plugged into a Windows 2000 system. The role of WSH is to take a script file and associated parameters, pass them to the appropriate language interpreter, and arrange for the necessary windows (or input and output files) to be accessible to the script. Microsoft will supply interpreters for Microsoft Visual Basic Scripting Edition (aka VBScript), JavaScript, and Microsoft JScript. They are working with other product developers to make sure that popular interpreted languages such as Perl and REXX are also available for Windows 2000.

How WMI and WSH Interact

Figure 4-1 illustrates the major components we've described and shows some of the basic ways in which they interact. Notice that WMI communicates with lower levels to gather information from drivers. WMI does not interact directly with the user; it relies on other applications to display the management information. The role of WSH is to provide support for custom scripts that automate administrative operations. Later in the chapter, we'll look at a couple of detailed examples of WSH scripts in action.

Windows Management Instrumentation

WMI is specific to the Windows platform and is not intended for use on other operating systems. Currently, Windows 98 and Windows 2000 support the Windows Driver Model (WDM) for interaction between the operating system and the hardware. WDM drivers support the WMI interfaces, but the vendor that supplies the driver must write that driver specifically to take advantage of WMI. In addition, WMI supports a number of existing device drivers, such as the NDIS (Network Driver Interface Specification) network adapter class drivers and SCSI class drivers.

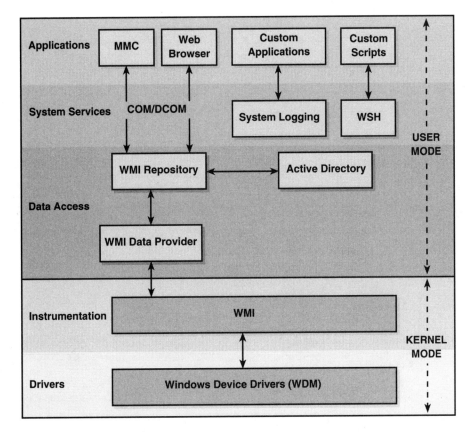

Figure 4-1.
How the WMI and WSH components interact.

WMI-enabled drivers utilize a Managed Object Format (MOF) file to record device information—error data, performance data, and the like. MOF is simply a formal way of defining attributes for entities in a managed environment. Windows 2000 incorporates a number of MOF definitions developed by Microsoft for common devices. WMI also allows a hardware manufacturer to extend these definitions (perhaps to support additional device capabilities) and to develop completely new MOF definitions for unsupported devices.

Another important capability of WMI is its support for device configuration operations. With this feature, the administrator can use a management application to configure a device using the WMI interface rather than having to configure the device manually. Figure 4-2 on the following page shows how the components of the WMI subsystem interact.

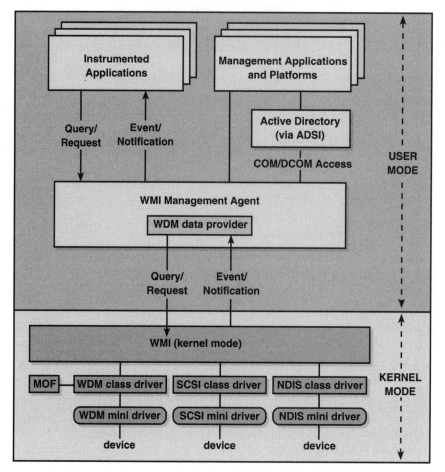

Figure 4-2.
Components of the WMI subsystem and their interaction.

Windows Scripting Host

The Windows Scripting Host is a language-independent subsystem that allows scripts to be written and executed on any 32-bit Windows system. A script is a series of commands that the computer reads and executes. Scripts differ from programs because they are *interpreted*, rather than compiled. Interpreted scripts are not converted to the computer's internal language until they are actually executing. Compiled programs are stored in binary format, while scripts are normally stored in text format. This format makes it easier for administrators to make quick modifications to a script.

Although its primary use will probably be on a Windows 2000 platform, versions of WSH are available for Windows NT 4.0 and Windows 98. You can use WSH in any scenario that requires a script—for example, logon and logoff processing, system configurations, and routine administrative operations. Finally the aging MS-DOS command language can be retired.

In operation, WSH is rather simple. You prepare a script in your language of choice and run a command from a command prompt, such as

```
cscript //T:30 simplescript.vbs /disk=D:
```

This command tells the command line version of WSH (cscript.exe) to run simplescript.vbs with a timeout period of 30 seconds (to allow the system to terminate an apparently inactive script), passing the script the parameter "disk=D:". Notice the differentiation of parameters in this command line—the double slash "//" denotes parameters specific to cscript.exe, whereas the single slash "/" denotes script parameters. The command line might seem complicated—fortunately, you can create shortcuts for commonly used scripts.

> NOTE: There are several other standard parameters that control script operation. You can find details on these parameters at *http://msdn.microsoft.com/scripting*.

There is an associated version of WSH (wscript.exe) that runs within the Windows graphical environment. You would usually invoke scripts in this environment either by using the Windows Run command from the Start menu or simply by double-clicking the script file. In either case, the role of WSH is to arrange the invocation of the appropriate language interpreter, pass the script and its parameters to the interpreter, and set up the screen or window where the script interpreter can display its output.

The WSH Programming Model

Writing scripts within the WSH environment is different from writing batch files. You must understand the WSH object model to create more than a very simple script. Fortunately, if you have experience using JScript, Visual Basic, or any object-oriented programming language, you're already familiar with the model. On the following page is a simple VBScript that creates a shell and displays the environment variables.

```
' SHOWVAR.VBS
'
' This example will list all the current environment variables.

' Initialize the shell object.
Dim WSHShell
Set WSHShell = WScript.CreateObject("WScript.Shell")

' Initialize variables.
intIndex = 0
strText = ""
intNumEnv = 0
MAX_ENV = 20
CRLF = Chr(13) & Chr(10)

' Loop through each environment variable.
For Each strEnv In WSHShell.Environment("PROCESS")
    intIndex = intIndex + 1
    ' Format the variable for display.
    strText = strText & CRLF & Right("    " & intIndex, 4) & _
        " " & strEnv
    intNumEnv = intNumEnv + 1
    ' Display the variable in a message box.
    If intNumEnv >= MAX_ENV Then
        MsgBox strText, vbInformation, "SHOWVAR.VBS"
        strText = ""
        intNumEnv = 0
    End If
Next

' Display any remaining values.
If intNumEnv >= 1 Then MsgBox strText, vbInformation, "SHOWVAR.VBS"
```

A few points about this example help illustrate some of the power underlying the WSH environment:

- Every script, by default, has access to a WScript object. Methods and properties of the WScript object provide the doorways to the rest of the system. Examples of simple methods are *echo*, to display text on screen, and *quit*, to terminate a script.

- The *CreateObject* call is one important method defined for the WScript object. It allows the invocation of other OLE automation objects. This applies not just to simple objects such as the shell object used in this example, but to *any* OLE automation server on the system. Thus, you can invoke and control Microsoft Word, Microsoft

Excel, or indeed any application registered as an automation server. This capability alone gives the scripting environment of Windows 2000 Server tremendous power.

- Under Windows 2000, the WSH environment supports an Active Directory object (but, obviously, not under Windows NT 4.0, Windows 95, or Windows 98). This interface allows Windows 2000 scripts access to all the information maintained by the directory. Active Directory plays a central role in Windows 2000, so this interface opens up tremendous possibilities for writing simple, powerful, customized administrative tools.

Let's look at a more complex example that illustrates some of these points. The script below illustrates both the use of Automation and the Active Directory interface. The script takes a single parameter (the name of a Microsoft Excel spreadsheet file), invokes Excel, reads a list of users' details from the spreadsheet, and then registers these users on the system using the Active Directory Service Interfaces (ADSI). The format of the spreadsheet for this example is shown in Table 4-1 on page 57. It contains the Directory Services (DS) root as well as the name, e-mail address, and organizational unit information for each of the users we want to register on the local system.

```
' ADDUSERS.VBS
'
' This script adds users using ADSI.
' The script reads an Excel spreadsheet that contains a list
' of users to add.
'
' The sample uses the directory root
' "LDAP://DC=Acme,DC=Com,O=Internet".
'
    Dim oXL
    Dim u
    Dim c
    Dim root
    Dim ou
    Dim TextXL
    Dim oArgs

    ' Get the command line arguments.
    ' First argument is the file containing the list of users.
    Set oArgs = WScript.arguments

    TextXL = oArgs.item(0)
```

(continued)

```
        If (oArgs.Count = 0) Or (TextXL = "") Then
            WScript.Echo "No input file given. Stopping now."
            WScript.Quit(1)
        End If

        ' We will use ou to control loop; set initial value to null.
        ou = ""

        ' Start Excel.
        Set oXL = WScript.CreateObject("EXCEL.application")

        ' Open the workbook specified in the command line.
        oXL.workbooks.open TextXL

        ' Activate the worksheet named "Add".
        oXL.sheets("Add").Activate

        ' Put the cursor in the starting cell, and read the DS root.
        oXL.ActiveSheet.range("A2").Activate ' this cell has the DS root
        ' This is the starting point in the DS.
        root = oXL.activecell.Value

        ' Step to the next row.
        oXL.activecell.offset(1, 0).Activate

        ' Until we run out of data.
        Do While oXL.activecell.Value <> ""

            ' If the requested ou is a new one...
            If oXL.activecell.Value <> ou Then
                ' Pick up the ou name...
                ou = oXL.activecell.Value

                ' Compose the ADSI path...
                s = "LDAP://" + ou + "," + root

                ' And get the object.
                Set c = GetObject(s)
            End If

            ' User's common name from first and last names...
            uname = "CN=" + oXL.activecell.offset(0, 1).Value + " " _
                + oXL.activecell.offset(0, 2).Value

            ' Create the new user object...
            Set u = c.Create("user", uname)
```

```
' Set the properties of the new user...
u.Put "givenName", oXL.activecell.offset(0, 1).Value  'First
u.Put "sn", oXL.activecell.offset(0, 2).Value          'Last
u.Put "mail", oXL.activecell.offset(0, 3).Value        'Email
u.Put "SAMAccountName", oXL.activecell.offset(0, 4).Value 'SAM

' Enable the account; set to "must change password at logon"...
u.Put "userAccountControl",16

' And update the DS.
u.SetInfo

' Done with this object; discard it.
Set u = Nothing

' Step to the next user...
oXL.activecell.offset(1, 0).Activate    'Next row
Loop

' Done.  Close spreadsheet.
oXL.application.quit
```

ADDUSERS.VBS Script Spreadsheet

DS Root	First Name	Last Name	E-Mail Address	SAM Account
DC=Acme, DC=Com, O=Internet				
OU=TestOU1	Edward	Teach	EdwardTeach@acme.com	EdwardTeach
OU=TestOU1	Jean	LaFitte	JeanLaFitte@acme.com	JeanLafitte
OU=TestOU1	Henry	Morgan	HenryMorgan@acme.com	HenryMorgan
OU=TestOU1	Ida	May	IdaMay@acme.com	IdaMay

Table 4-1.
The results of running the ADDUSERS.VBS script.

Summary

In this chapter, we looked at the new, lower-level system management capability incorporated into Windows 2000: the Windows Management Interface. WMI allows applications to gather information from drivers, providing powerful performance and reliability monitoring. Applications can also use WMI to configure drivers. While some support is provided for legacy hardware, new drivers must be created specifically to take advantage of WMI. So don't expect everything to be WMI-compliant the day that Windows 2000 ships.

We also looked at the Windows Scripting Host environment. WSH provides the framework for scripts to run on a Windows 98 or Windows 2000 system. Given the capabilities of WSH, scripting using VBScript and other languages is bound to become much more popular. If you haven't already learned VBScript and the associated object model, take some time to learn it—scripting will make you a more effective administrator.

PART III

NETWORKING AND COMMUNICATIONS

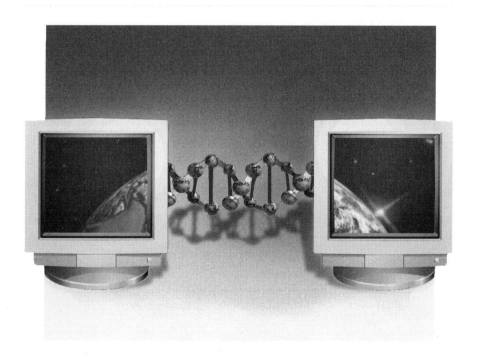

Security

Overview

Modern organizations rely on computer networks for their most important information. A good administrator can set up a network to share this information among users with little difficulty. However, it is much more challenging to ensure that *only* your users have access to their data. The challenge in securing a network is in allowing access for valid users while keeping information away from hackers.

Microsoft Windows 2000 Server provides the most sophisticated standards-based network security system available. It relies on certificates to identify both users and services, and provides all the software necessary for maintaining certification authority. It provides standards-based Kerberos version 5 authentication protocol integrated into Active Directory, guaranteeing users a single sign-on to their network. The new support for smart cards gives administrators new choices for authenticating their users. Finally, the encrypted file system keeps data safe on a disk, even if the computer is not physically secure.

This chapter will discuss the security features of the Windows 2000 family and introduce the services included with Windows 2000 Server.

Public/Private Key Pair Security Overview

Any business transaction depends on each party knowing the identity of the other party. If you purchase something with a credit card, your signature is compared against the signature already present on the card. This comparison is a form of authentication—theoretically, only you are able to produce a signature exactly like the one on the card.

Historically, proving that a user should have access to resources on a network has been a simple task. LANs (local area networks) without external access often trusted any user who had access to the resources. This system assumed that if the user had physical access to the building, he or she must be legitimate. Authenticating users based on their source IP address or domain name provides more protection, but sophisticated attacks can bypass that minimal security.

The modern networking environment is virtual in its very nature. Many networks can be accessed from anywhere on the Internet—and from anywhere in the world. Users must be identified beyond a doubt, and the messages they send must be guaranteed as genuine.

Man-in-the-middle attacks, in which servers are impersonated as illustrated in Figure 5-1, are also a concern. Such an attack can be avoided only if the server *and* the user both can prove their identities.

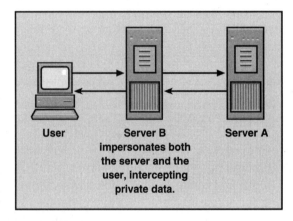

Figure 5-1.
To avoid man-in-the-middle attacks, both the user and the server must be sure of each other's identity.

Traditionally, usernames and passwords are used to identify users to servers. The server maintains a database of the passwords, which it compares against the information sent by the user to confirm the user's knowledge of the password. The user and the server have shared knowledge of the private password. Operating systems such as Microsoft Windows NT transmit and store this data in an encrypted format, making it difficult or impossible to intercept and misuse. This method worked well to identify users but did nothing to verify the identity of servers.

Public key security provides a better way of identifying resources on networks. The technology works on the principle of *key pairs*. A key pair consists of a public key and a private key, and though the two are closely related, it is impossible to derive one from the other. In other words, the public key can be freely traded without concern that someone could determine the private key from it.

These keys have a special relationship. When data is encrypted using the public key, it can only be decrypted using the private key. The encryption process is only one-way when a single key is possessed—it is impossible to encrypt a file using the public key, and then decrypt it again with that same key. The relationship between keys in a key pair has significant implications for network security.

A Story to Illustrate Key Pairs

Consider the following scenario: Pete needs to send a shopping list to Erica. It is important that the message remain confidential and that Erica receive it exactly as it was sent. Some bad people would like to intercept this message, add an item to the list, and send it on its way.

Pete can ensure that the list is not modified in transit by encrypting it with Erica's public key. Pete will also use his private key to add a digital signature to the message. Both Erica and the bad people have the public key, but only Erica has the private key that is required for decryption. Erica is sure that the message was sent by Pete because she can use Pete's public key to verify his signature. The message's integrity is guaranteed, and the sender is authenticated.

This scenario was somewhat simplified. There is a lot of overhead to encrypting an entire message, so a summary of the message would have been created, digitally signed, and attached to the end of the message. Encryption of large amounts of data is not done using public keys. Instead, the message itself would have been encrypted using a symmetric algorithm.

For the key pair to be useful, there must be some way of guaranteeing that the key is valid. Anyone can generate a key pair with correct software, so it only becomes useful for authentication if an organization can guarantee that it belongs to a particular person or company. These organizations are known as Certification Authorities (CA). The most well known CA is Verisign, a company that has been issuing certificates for several years.

To summarize how this works, Certification Authorities are responsible for validating the identity of a person or organization and associating that entity with a key pair. The CA will store the public key and maintain a list of certificates issued. Data encrypted with the public key can only be decrypted using the private key. Therefore, key pairs can be used to verify identity. However, Certification Authorities must be trusted in order to identify the entity in the first place.

Kerberos Protocol

The Kerberos protocol is an Internet standard for authentication. Kerberos version 5 authentication protocol is supported by Windows 2000 server and is defined in Internet Engineering Task Force (IETF) RFC 1510. It is now the native authentication method for Windows 2000 systems. Any Active Directory server automatically has the Kerberos Key Distribution Center (KDC) service running, and all Windows 2000 systems support the protocol as a client.

Kerberos authentication is based on *tickets*. This is analogous to buying a ticket to an amusement park. Once you pay for and receive the ticket, you can go anywhere in the park, as many times as you like, until you leave. The Kerberos ticket is entirely encrypted and contains enough information to identify the user and verify his or her authentication.

Kerberos authentication has an advantage over traditional Windows NT authentication. When a user logged in to a Windows NT 4.0 network, he or she would be authenticated upon login by a domain controller. Then, every network resource the user accessed would need to issue a separate authentication request to a domain controller. The Kerberos protocol issues a ticket to the client system. The ticket is used to validate the user to the network resource being accessed, and it also validates the network resource to the client. Therefore, the Kerberos protocol protects against the possibility of impersonating a server.

The Kerberos protocol is an improvement over other methods of authentication simply because it is an Internet standard. While Windows 2000 clients and servers will be the easiest to administer, any client or server that supports the Kerberos protocol can participate. This reduces the amount of infrastructure that must be supported in heterogeneous networks because the same authentication servers can validate both UNIX and Windows 2000 clients. Administrators do not need in-depth knowledge of the workings of the Kerberos protocol because it is handled transparently by the operating system.

SSPI (Security Support Provider Interface)

Developers can take advantage of the SSPI, the Security Support Provider Interface, to create applications that leverage the security protocols built in to Windows 2000 Server. SSPI provides an application interface that can create authenticated connections. The specific method used for authentication is hidden from the application, allowing administrators to choose from a variety of Security Support Providers (SSP) without being concerned with compatibility.

Windows NT 4.0 shipped with the Microsoft Windows NT LAN Manager (NTLM) SSP. Windows 2000 Server ships with the Microsoft Kerberos protocol SSP. Once they become available, other SSPs can be used as well. If an application makes use of the SSPI, it will be compatible with any SSP implemented in the future.

Certificate and Key Management

Several aspects of Windows 2000 security depend on certificates. The MMC Certificates snap-in, shown in Figure 5-2, is an administrative tool used to manage these keys and to specify which Certification Authorities to trust. Any certificates with associated private keys that reside on the system are manageable using this utility. Applications and services can then use these certificates as part of their security structure.

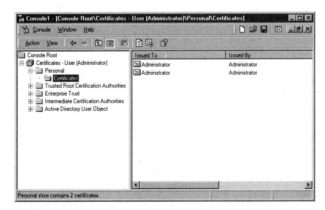

Figure 5-2.
The Certificates snap-in handles certificates that reside on your system.

Windows 2000 is the first Windows operating system to offer centralized certificate management. Previous versions of Windows relied on individual applications to maintain their own keys and a list of trusted CAs. Several Microsoft applications, such as Internet Explorer, used the registry to store certificate and CA information—but third-party applications had to be managed independently. The new architecture and management utilities will increase the usefulness of certificates, thereby increasing the overall security of your network.

If you create your own Certification Authority, you will want to import its certificate to add it as a trusted CA using the Certificates snap-in. This creates a trust for only a specific user; use the Group Policy to make changes that affect multiple users. As shown in Figure 5-3, many of the commercial CAs are trusted by default. Any CA that you do not want to trust should be removed from all systems on your network.

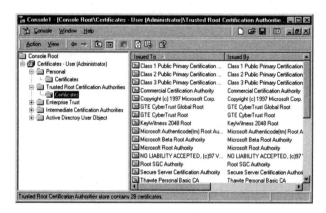

Figure 5-3.
The Certificates snap-in allows CAs to be added and removed from the trusted list.

Security Templates

Maintaining the security of an entire network of machines can be a difficult task. To make that task more manageable, Windows 2000 Server includes Security Templates. This tool allows administrators to create security templates that specify various settings on a machine. These templates can be applied to a single system or an entire network of computers running Windows 2000. Security Templates can even be used to analyze the security on a system to determine what aspects of the system do not meet company standards.

Security Templates is an MMC snap-in utility. To use it, launch an MMC console and add it in manually. Security Templates, shown in Figure 5-4, will seem familiar if you have used the Group Policy tool, because they provide similar functionality. The two tools are very different, however. Security Templates modifies security templates, which later can be applied to a group or user. The Group Policy tool, on the other hand, actively changes a group's or user's settings.

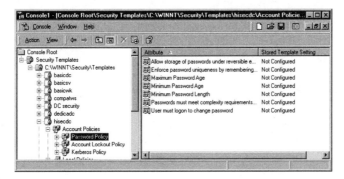

Figure 5-4.
Security Templates allows you to create security templates that can be applied to Windows 2000 systems.

A handful of templates are provided with the standard Windows 2000 server distribution. By default, templates are provided for basic and high levels of security on Windows 2000 Professional, Windows 2000 Server, and domain controller systems. It is a good idea to use these templates as a starting point for your own templates. While these templates might not suit your organization exactly, they can save you time compared with creating a new template from scratch. Templates are stored in a simple text file. By default, these files have an .inf extension and are stored in the *systemroot*\security\templates\ directory. To use an existing template as the basis for a custom template, simply copy the file within that directory and edit it using Security Templates.

Security Templates is used to modify security settings that previously required using several different tools: User Manager, Event Viewer, Windows Explorer, and the Registry Editor. By opening a security template and expanding the Account Policies tree, you can modify settings such as the password age, length, and complexity. The Local Policies tree, displayed in the Security

Templates in Figure 5-5, contains auditing settings, user rights, and security options. Event log settings can also be included in security templates.

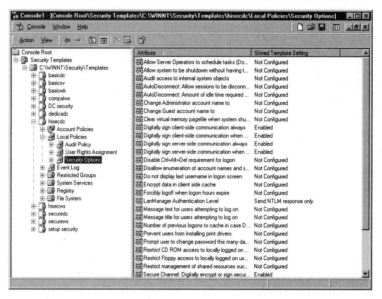

Figure 5-5.
Security Templates can modify settings that previously required using many different tools.

Security templates are flexible and can identify specific objects that exist on systems or within Active Directory. The registry tree, displayed in Security Templates in Figure 5-6, is used to ensure that specific registry keys have the correct permissions. This allows administrators to enforce security for the keys they find most important without attempting to declare a policy for every single key within the registry. You can choose whether you want the permissions to be applied to objects deeper in the tree hierarchy. Similarly, policies can be set for specific files and folders on the file system and specific objects and containers within Active Directory.

Security Configuration and Analysis Tool

The Security Configuration and Analysis tool is a companion to Security Templates. It is an MMC snap-in that must be added manually to a console. It is used to apply the restrictions in security templates to actual systems, and is capable of analyzing the security of systems. After an analysis is initiated, it will take several minutes to audit the security of the system. This process is shown in Figure 5-7.

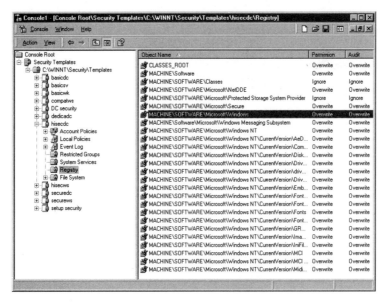

Figure 5-6.
Security on specific objects within the registry, file system, and Active Directory can be enforced.

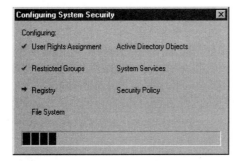

Figure 5-7.
The Security Configuration and Analysis tool audits the security of systems according to the rules you specify.

The results of the analysis are written to a text file that is automatically displayed once the analysis is complete. This text file, shown in Figure 5-8, indicates to the administrator whether the audit was successful and shows where any errors occurred.

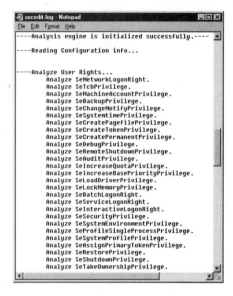

Figure 5-8.
The results of a security configuration analysis are stored in a text file and displayed upon completion.

Certificate Services

Many administrators would like to guarantee the identity of users within their organization without purchasing key pairs from an outside CA. Becoming your own CA is not only cost effective but also extremely secure. After all, you know your own employees better than any outside organization does. Assigning certificates to all users and services on the network ensures secure, transparent access regardless of the user's location.

Installing Certificate Services

Windows 2000 Server ships with all the necessary software you need to be a Certification Authority. Simply choose to install Certificate Services during the installation of the operating system. You can also add the service later by choosing Add/Remove Programs from Control Panel and selecting Windows Components.

When you install Certificate Services, you will need to choose what level of CA services you want to provide. As shown in Figure 5-9, you have four choices:

- Enterprise root CA. This is the correct option if you are using Active Directory and this is the first CA in your organization.

- Enterprise subordinate CA. Choose this option if you use Active Directory but this is not the first CA.

- Stand-alone root CA. This should be selected if it is the first CA and Active Directory is not in use.

- Stand-alone subordinate CA. For organizations that already have a CA structure but are not using Active Directory.

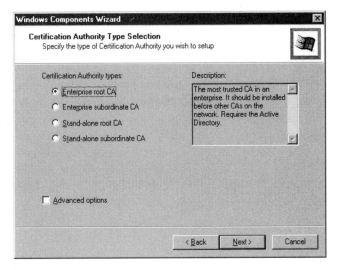

Figure 5-9.
Certificate Services works with or without Active Directory and can participate in a hierarchy of servers.

After you choose the role your Certificate Services will play in your CA hierarchy, select the cryptography provider, hash algorithm, and key length. (A discussion of the pros and cons of each of these technologies would be quite lengthy and well outside the scope of this book.) Once that decision has been made, you will need to identify your new CA with information about your organization, as shown in Figure 5-10. This identifying information is very important because it will be added to every certificate you create and used to identify certificates as belonging to you.

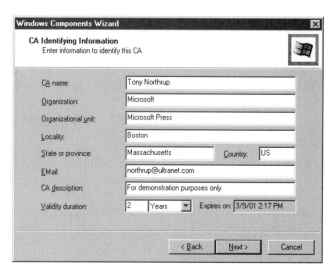

Figure 5-10.
Every certificate you create includes information identifying the CA.

After you have entered the identifying information for the CA, you will need to specify a location for the files to be stored. Be sure to choose a partition formatted with the version of the NTFS file system used in Windows 2000. If you are creating an enterprise-root or enterprise-subordinate CA, you will need to define the types of certificates the CA can issue. This is done using the Certificate Services MMC snap-in. With Certificate Services installed, you are ready to issue and validate certificates!

Managing Certificate Services

Certificate Services is managed using the Certification Authority MMC snap-in. An icon for the tool is available within the Administrative Tools folder in the Programs group of the Start menu. This tool is simple to use and allows administrators to view certificates that have been issued, revoked, requested, or rejected. You can also view the certificate that validates the Certificate Services as a Certification Authority. The Certification Authority snap-in is shown in Figure 5-11.

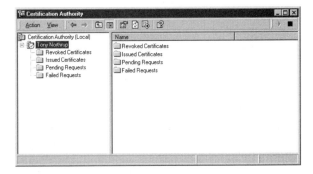

Figure 5-11.
The Certification Authority snap-in is used to manage certificate requests.

Smart Cards

User name and password authentication techniques are no longer sufficient for many organizations. One of the most interesting new trends is the smart card. A smart card identifies the user who carries it, utilizing unique information provided by the card or stored within the card.

A typical smart card—the size of a credit card—stores information about a user and might contain a microprocessor. The user first authenticates himself to the smart card using a personal identification number (PIN). Only the user assigned to the smart card will know that PIN, guaranteeing that the user being authenticated has both the physical card and the required knowledge. Then, the smart card can authenticate the user to the operating system using the Kerberos authentication protocol. This process allows the user to be validated without entering any form of a password into the computer.

Using smart cards is superior to using passwords for several reasons:

- The risk of an attacker misusing a password is eliminated.

- A physical item, the smart card itself, is required for authentication.

- A PIN must be entered into the smart card, ensuring that it is being used by the proper person.

- No form of the password or any reusable information is entered into a computer or transmitted over the network.

- A user can carry electronic credentials for use at work, at home, or while traveling.

Magnetic strip cards are similar to smart cards, but cost less and lack the processing capability. The magnetic strip can contain a great deal of information to identify a user and can even hold a private key. Magnetic strip cards require a greater hardware investment than self-contained smart cards, because all the users' systems must have smart magnetic strip card readers.

Windows NT 4.0 required administrators to add third-party software onto the system to allow smart cards to authenticate users. Software developers had a difficult time integrating smart cards into Windows NT because the authentication methods were not very flexible, and it was impractical to protect every method of accessing the system.

Windows 2000 includes smart card capabilities integrated into the operating system. Additionally, the flexible authentication methods ensure that software developers can easily integrate their custom applications into the user environment.

Encrypting File System (EFS)

The Encrypting File System (EFS) protects files on NTFS partitions from being accessed outside of Windows 2000 security. While Windows 2000 guarantees that only authenticated users can access files they have been granted access to, it is possible to boot a system to another operating system. Another operating system is capable of disregarding the access control lists associated with the files and granting unauthorized users read and write access to unencrypted files.

EFS encrypts the file on the disk using public/private key pair technology. The user must have access to the private key to have access to the file. When Windows 2000 is running, it acts as an additional layer of file security.

For more information on EFS, please refer to Chapter 3, "Zero Administration for Windows."

Summary

Windows 2000 Server provides the most secure standards-based Internet and networking environment available. The proprietary authentication method used with Windows NT networks has been replaced with Kerberos version 5 authentication protocol. The Kerberos protocol is capable of authenticating both the user *and* the server, reducing the risk of a malicious hacker impersonating the server system.

Public/private key pair certificates are now integrated into the operating system. The Group Policy, Certificates, and Certificate Services MMC snap-ins can be used to view and remove certificates and Certification Authorities. Certificate Services allows a Windows 2000 Server to become a CA and participate in a CA hierarchy. Because it is integrated into Active Directory, Certificate Services can be distributed and redundant.

The new security architecture allows for greater flexibility. Support for smart cards, an increasingly common method of authenticating users, is now built in to the operating system. Applications developers can make use of SSPI to establish connections based on whichever authentication method the administrator has chosen. Administrators of heterogeneous networks will benefit because UNIX systems can act as both authentication clients and servers.

Security features will only benefit organizations that make use of them. Fortunately, Microsoft has provided user-friendly interfaces for every technology. While the underlying protocols involved in each of these technologies can be difficult to understand, they are easy to administer using the MMC interfaces.

Network Infrastructure

Overview

Developed from the start as a network operating system, Microsoft Windows 2000 Server continues to improve its presence on networks and the Internet. Microsoft is following the worldwide trend of using the Internet for as much as possible.

Windows 2000 Server will help companies make better use of their Internet connections. By providing support for additional standardized features of TCP/IP, Microsoft has improved the performance of its premier network operating system both for communications with other Windows systems and with UNIX systems. Technologies such as virtual private networks (VPNs) will allow organizations to reduce costs without sacrificing security. The routing features built in to Windows 2000 servers allow those servers to act as routers, with graphical user interfaces far superior to those of hardware-based routers. The new Quality of Service (QoS) standards allow more consistent and reliable networking, especially when using real-time audio and video.

Support for Standards

With the first releases of the LAN Manager and Windows NT operating systems, Microsoft made an effort not only to support Internet standards but also to create its own protocols where standards did not meet the needs of its customers. NetBIOS Enhanced User Interface (NetBEUI), the networking foundation of the first versions of Windows NT, was proprietary in nature and the details of the protocol were well hidden. TCP/IP, on the contrary, is based entirely on committee-created, completely documented standards. TCP/IP is the standard of the Internet and the future of networking, and Windows 2000 is well designed to leverage these standards.

Microsoft is not simply following open standards; it is leading the development. For example, Microsoft has been working with Cisco, Ascend, IBM, and 3Com to create the Layer 2 Tunneling Protocol (L2TP) standards. Microsoft's active involvement in standards committees ensures that Windows will take advantage of these technologies just as soon as they are finalized—and sometimes before!

TCP/IP Improvements

While the core of TCP/IP (Transmission Control Protocol/Internet Protocol) has been a standard for many years, not all TCP/IP implementations are alike. Many aspects of TCP/IP are considered optional, and software developers tend to add only those features they feel will benefit their customers. Microsoft has improved the TCP/IP stack included in Windows 2000 by adding optional, standardized features not found in previous versions of Windows. The end result is that users will enjoy improved network performance on both local area networks (LANs) and wide area networks (WANs).

Security-minded administrators will appreciate the new support for robust packet filtering. Windows 2000 can now filter packets based on TCP port, UDP port, IP protocol ID, ICMP type, ICMP code, source address, and destination address. An example of packet filtering is shown in Figure 6-1. With these filtering capabilities, you can control which networks are allowed to download mail from your Post Office Protocol (POP) server. This control would allow you to guarantee that only users on the local network can even attempt to establish network connections.

Filter lists make it easier to manage multiple filtering policies. Figure 6-2 shows how several lists can be used to provide separate policies for internal and external networks. You can create separate filters for each subnet in your network, if you so desire.

Windows 2000 now includes support for RFCs 1122, 1123, 1323, and Selective Acknowledgements. RFCs 1122 and 1123 were written in 1989 and summarize mandatory and optional features of TCP/IP stacks—support for these documents means better compatibility with other operating systems. RFC 1323 provides extensions to TCP that allow for better performance over high-bandwidth and high-delay networks, such as satellite links. Selective Acknowledgements improve performance when used with large TCP window sizes, by allowing only lost packets to be resent; packets that were already received are not retransmitted. For more information on Selective Acknowledgements, refer to RFC 2018.

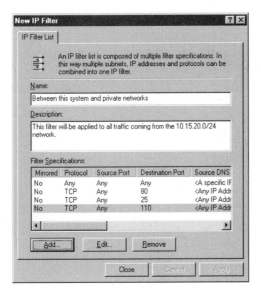

Figure 6-1.
Windows 2000 allows packet filtering based on IP address and port number.

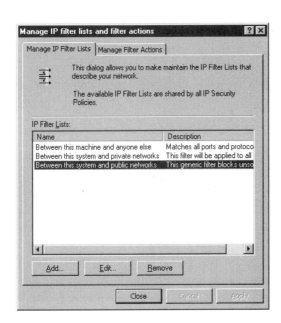

Figure 6-2.
Multiple filters can be grouped together and managed as policies.

Windows 2000 Server continues Microsoft's support of the Winsock 2.0 interface. Winsock provides an API for Internet applications and automatically handles tasks such as name resolution, QoS, establishing outgoing connections, and listening for incoming connections. Winsock 2.0 allows applications to specify QoS requirements, regardless of the underlying QoS mechanism in use.

Virtual Private Networks (VPNs)

A VPN allows data to travel securely across an untrusted network. In the Internet age, this means that companies that formerly required leased lines to ensure security can now leverage the public Internet for private communications. It also means that corporate users who travel can connect to a local Internet service provider (ISP) and communicate securely with the corporate network, without dialing in to a private bank of modems. See Figure 6-3 for an illustration of a VPN across the public Internet.

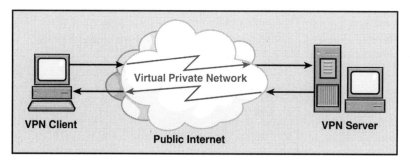

Figure 6-3.
A virtual private network carries data securely across a public network.

The primary advantages of VPNs are reduced costs and improved privacy. Companies can reduce costs by maintaining only a single WAN connection for each remote office—a connection to an ISP. The ISP forwards the traffic across the public Internet, in much the same way that frame relay providers have operated for many years, except at a greatly reduced cost. The VPN technologies included in Windows 2000 ensure that this data cannot be read or modified on its journey to the destination network.

While different VPN technologies vary in their specifics, they have many things in common. All VPNs transport data through a *tunnel,* as illustrated in Figure 6-4. The tunnel is created between two tunnel endpoints, which agree upon a set of protocols for the tunnel before any payload is transmitted. As data is sent through the tunnel, the frame or packet is *encapsulated* within another packet. Once the data reaches the opposite endpoint, the data is unencapsulated and processed as if it had been sent from a system on the same LAN.

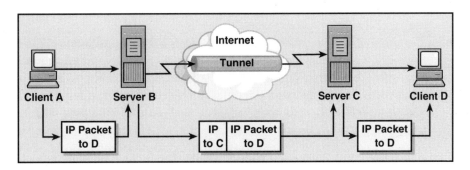

Figure 6-4.
Tunnels encapsulate data within IP packets.

Windows 2000 includes three technologies for creating virtual private networks. PPTP, the Point-to-Point Tunneling Protocol, is a familiar technology to those who have worked with Windows in the past. L2TP provides similar functionality but has the benefit of support from a variety of vendors. Internet Protocol security (IPSec) represents the future of tunneling. Though IPSec is still under development, Windows 2000 provides support for much of the published functionality.

Point-to-Point Tunneling Protocol (PPTP)

PPTP is a multiprotocol tunneling technology developed by Microsoft for Windows NT 4.0. It is based on the well-established Point-to-Point Protocol (PPP), which is used for the vast majority of dial-up connections. While PPP allows two computers to communicate over a single link, PPTP allows a *virtual* link to be created that can traverse public or private networks. PPTP was quick to develop because it borrows the authentication and handshaking mechanisms from PPP.

While only Windows NT 4.0 Server or Windows 2000 Server can act as the server end of a PPTP connection, any member of the Windows family can be a client. This allows traveling users to dial in to an ISP with a Windows 98 laptop and initiate a private connection across the Internet to the corporate server. This will work properly regardless of the protocol in use at the corporate network; the traveler can dial in to an ISP and connect to a NetWare server located on a private network, using only IPX/SPX.

Layer 2 Tunneling Protocol (L2TP)

L2TP, seen as an evolution of PPTP, is a multiprotocol tunneling technology developed by Microsoft, Cisco, Ascend, IBM, and 3Com. L2TP meets many of the same goals as PPTP and borrows heavily from Cisco's Layer-2 Forwarding (L2F).

One of the interesting features of L2TP is MPPP, or Multilink Point-to-Point Protocol. This differs from the MPPP technology built in to Windows NT 4.0. The MPPP built in to Windows NT 4.0 could be used only to connect to a dial-up server that specifically supported this technology. Unfortunately, the technology was not widely supported where it was needed most—by the ISPs. L2TP's MPPP technology allows a Windows 2000 system to dial in to two entirely separate ISP connections. Data can be transmitted through both of these links to a Windows 2000 server using L2TP MPPP, where the server will reassemble the traffic and transmit it onto the Internet or a private network. In this way, Windows 2000 Server and the L2TP MPPP allow multiple analog links to be combined for greater data throughput. This process is illustrated in Figure 6-5.

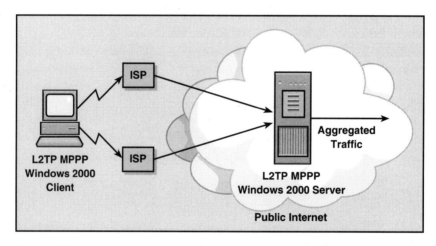

Figure 6-5.
L2TP allows multiple links to be aggregated.

L2TP offers other advantages over PPTP. L2TP can be used over a variety of Internet connections, including frame relay, X.25, and Asynchronous Transfer Mode (ATM). L2TP allows multiple tunnels to be created, each with a different QoS. Header compression in L2TP reduces the header to 4 bytes, compared to the 6 bytes PPTP uses.

Both L2TP and PPTP are configured and managed in Windows 2000 using the Routing And Remote Access service. Figure 6-6 shows a screen shot of the management utility.

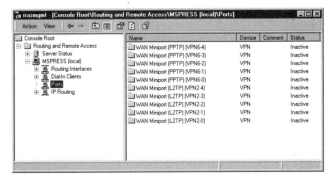

Figure 6-6.
The Routing And Remote Access service is used to configure L2TP and PPTP.

Windows Internet Protocol Security (IPSec)

One of the new standards that the Internet Engineering Task Force (IETF) has been working on is IPSec. The goal of the IPSec working group is to allow private and secure communications across the public Internet, regardless of the application or higher-level protocol being used. PPTP, L2TP, and several other technologies also accomplish these goals, but IPSec has one distinct advantage—it is an Internet standard. This single factor will allow IPSec to become one of the primary protocols used in VPNs in the years to come.

Microsoft, in a continuing effort to support international standards, has provided an implementation of IPSec in Windows 2000. When used with Windows 2000, IPSec provides transparent authentication of clients and servers, confidentiality of data transmitted across a network, and the flexibility to work with any IP-based application.

Encapsulating Security Payload (ESP) is IPSec's standard for encryption and validation. ESP operates at either the network layer or the transport layer of the Open Systems Interconnection (OSI) model, and therefore can encrypt data created by any higher-layer protocols. For example, a Telnet session could be tunneled within ESP, and all data transmitted during that Telnet session would be immune to eavesdropping. When ESP is used at the transport layer, an ESP header is inserted between the IP header and the TCP header. The TCP header information and all data contained within the packet are encrypted.

ESP can also be used at the network layer to provide VPN functionality and privacy. When ESP is used at the network layer, the exact IP address of the packets can be obscured. In this way, data can travel between remote networks, but the IP addresses within the networks will not be revealed to anyone watching the traffic.

The encryption ensures that the traffic cannot be monitored and used maliciously. Further, ESP provides protection from replay attacks by providing a sequencing number within the header. A *replay attack* is a scenario wherein an unauthorized user retransmits packets that had been intercepted. Windows Internet Protocol security leverages the Internet Security Association and Key Management Protocol (ISAKMP) using the Oakley key determination protocol to identify each packet uniquely and ensure that it can never be reused. Figure 6-7 shows an event log entry generated by an error associated with ISAKMP/Oakley.

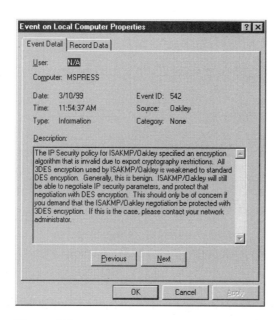

Figure 6-7.
IPSec uses ISAKMP with the Oakley key determination protocol.

The other significant standard being designed by the IPSec working group is the IP Authentication Header, or simply AH. AH allows the client and server to validate each other before they begin to exchange data, limiting the opportunity for a malicious third party to impersonate either end of the connection. AH and ESP together provide authentication and encryption of IP traffic.

The IETF provided a framework for data encryption and session authentication using the ESP and AH standards. It did not provide standards for the actual mechanisms used to encrypt the data or to authenticate the hosts. Fortunately, Microsoft has built a strong authentication mechanism into Windows 2000 Server—client and server certificates. The encryption is provided by mixing public key and secret key cryptography. By leveraging existing components of Windows 2000 Server, Microsoft has provided an easy-to-use and powerful method of network security.

NOTE: Figure 6-8 shows how administrators can configure custom IPSec security policies using the IP Security Policies MMC snap-in. If protocols other than IP must be tunneled, IPSec can be combined with L2TP. For more information on IPSec standards, please visit the IETF's Web site at *http://www.ietf.org/html.charters/ ipsec-charter.html.*

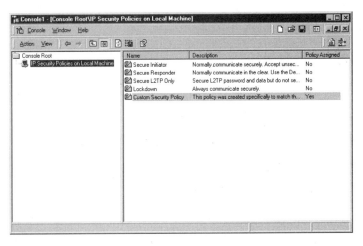

Figure 6-8.
Set custom IPSec policies with the IP Security Policies MMC snap-in.

Network Driver Interface Specification (NDIS)

NDIS is a layer of abstraction that exists between the network protocol driver (at the network layer of the OSI model) and the network card driver (at the data link layer of the OSI model). Among other features, it allows multiple network cards to work with a single network protocol. NDIS is an international standard, and providing NDIS support allows network card vendors to ensure that their driver will be compatible with Windows.

Both Windows 98 and Windows 2000 provide native support for NDIS 5.0. This is an upgrade from Windows NT 4.0 and Windows 95 (OSR2), which shipped with NDIS 4.0 support. NDIS 5.0 adds several features that were absent in NDIS 4.0:

- Advanced network power management and network wake-up capabilities.
- Plug and Play is now supported with network drivers.
- Improved performance.
- Improved support for ATM and QoS.
- Lower total cost of ownership (TCO).

Routing

Microsoft has built routing functionality into its server operating systems since Windows NT 3.51 was released. However, the multiprotocol router (MPR) built in to Windows NT 3.51 and Windows NT 4.0 was limited in functionality and found very little use on production networks. Microsoft recognized the need for a flexible, extensible routing technology, and began developing a replacement for the built-in routing in Windows NT 4.0. Windows 2000 Server continues to build on Windows NT's routing capabilities with the new Routing And Remote Access service.

With the routing functionality built in to Windows 2000 Server, Microsoft allows organizations to build entire network infrastructures based strictly on Microsoft products. By integrating routing features into the operating system, small companies will benefit by not having to purchase expensive routing hardware to segment networks. Large companies will benefit by being able to administer their routers using Windows 2000's graphical user interface (GUI), a major improvement over most routers' text-based interfaces.

Network Address Translation (NAT)

Network address translation, or NAT, is the process of transparently using a proxy to transfer packets between an internal and external network. With the NAT functionality built in to Windows 2000 Server, a single dial-up connection can be used to allow an entire network access to the Internet, without making a single change to the clients. Until now, administrators had to make use of application- or session-layer proxies, both of which require modifications to the client and support a limited number of applications.

For NAT to work properly, clients on the internal network must be using private IP addresses, such as those in the 192.168.0.0 range. The clients must have the NAT server configured as their default gateway. The NAT server will act as a router to the clients, forwarding packets from the internal network to the external network. However, NAT does more than a traditional router—it not only forwards the packets, it replaces the private source IP address with a valid public IP address. NAT also listens for reply packets and returns those responses to the client that initiated the connection.

Beyond providing outside access to clients within a private network, the NAT services included with Windows 2000 Server are also capable of acting as a reverse-proxy. This allows administrators to create publicly available Web and e-mail services without placing the servers on a public network. NAT can also be configured to use a range of public IP addresses, assign clients private IP addresses using Dynamic Host Configuration Protocol (DHCP), and act as a proxy for DNS (Domain Name System) requests to the outside world. All of these features combined allow administrators to easily provide a private network access to the public Internet or any other network.

NAT is configured using the Routing And Remote Access MMC snap-in. It is treated as a routing protocol, though it is not a true routing protocol. Enabling NAT can be as simple as adding the protocol and selecting the proper radio button, as shown in Figure 6-9.

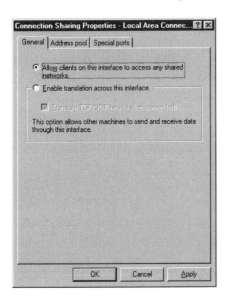

Figure 6-9.
The Routing And Remote Access MMC snap-in makes configuring network address translation simple.

Static Routing

Routers forward traffic one *hop* at a time. For a router to correctly forward traffic in networks where multiple paths exist, the router must be configured to know where the next hop is for any given destination network. Routing protocols allow routers to automatically learn their way around a network, but routing protocols require administrative overhead and may not be worthwhile in small networks and networks that do not require dynamic redundancy. If an administrator wants to manually configure each router in a network with a list of paths to different destination networks, he or she can do so using static routing.

Static routing is useful in small networks and extremely stable networks. Static routes can be configured on a Windows 2000 Server using the ROUTE command-line interface or the Routing And Remote Access GUI, as shown in Figure 6-10. For those familiar with the command-line interface included in previous versions of Windows, this graphical interface is a great improvement.

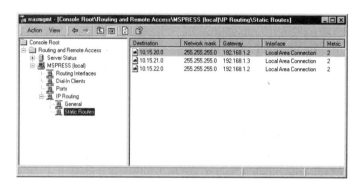

Figure 6-10.
Windows 2000 allows static routes to be configured within the Routing And Remote Access MMC snap-in.

Routing Protocols

In many small networks, all network segments connect to a single router. This router knows where to forward packets because it has a direct connection to every network segment. In this situation, only a very simple router is required. However, larger networks require multiple routers. This presents a bit of a challenge—how will the routers know where to forward packets that are not destined for directly attached networks? Consider Figure 6-11, which shows a network with two routers. Router A is directly connected to Networks W and X, and therefore knows how to forward packets from Network W destined for Network X. However, how will it know where to forward packets for Network Y or Network Z?

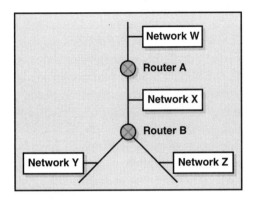

Figure 6-11.
Routing protocols are required so that routers will be aware of remote networks.

There are two correct answers to the question: either the network administrator can implement static routes, or a routing protocol can be used. A routing protocol enables Router B to tell Router A that it has a direct connection to Network Y and Network Z. That way, when Router A receives packets destined for Network Z, Router A will know to forward the packets directly to Router B for delivery.

For routers to exchange information about networks, they must use the same routing protocol. Routing protocols each have specific advantages and disadvantages. Windows 2000 Server includes support for a variety of routing protocols and provides an open API for the development of additional routing protocols. Using this open API, Microsoft or third-party vendors can write code that allows Windows 2000 servers to communicate with other routers on the network, regardless of the routing protocol.

The following section describes the routing protocols included with Windows 2000 Server: Routing Information Protocol (RIP) and Open Shortest Path First (OSPF).

RIP version 1, RIP version 2, and RIP for IPX

RIP (Routing Information Protocol) has been in use since 1982 and is still commonly used today. RIP is a member of the *distance-vector* routing protocol family. Distance-vector routing protocols learn a limited amount of information about the surrounding network and tend to suffer from problems such as routing loops. RIP version 1 is based on RFC 1058; RIP version 2 is based on RFC 1723.

While RIP is considered to be an outdated routing protocol, it is simple to configure and is widely supported by routing software. Many people still use

RIP for backward compatibility with older routers. Indeed, RIP was the only dynamic routing protocol supported by Windows NT 3.51.

You should use RIP only if you have to. If your organization requires the use of RIP as the routing protocol, RIP version 2 is the better choice. RIP version 2 has several advantages over RIP version 1. The newer version of the protocol allows classless networks to be used; RIP version 1 required that all subnets be divided into standard Class A, Class B, or Class C networks. While RIP version 1 sent all updates between routers on a timed basis, RIP version 2 sends updates only as required. Finally, RIP version 1 was susceptible to attacks because it lacked a method to authenticate other routers; RIP version 2 adds simple clear-text authentication.

RIP for IPX is a variant of the RIP standard, modified to work with Novell's native network protocol. It is the only routing protocol Windows 2000 Server supports that is compatible with IPX.

OSPF

OSPF (Open Shortest Path First) is a robust protocol, well suited to medium-to-large networks. It is a member of the *link-state* routing protocol family— a family characterized by complete knowledge of surrounding networks and sophisticated router-to-router communications. While distance-vector routing protocols such as RIP typically communicate only with directly neighboring routers, OSPF-based routers communicate with all other routers in their network. This allows the router to build a map of the network, providing for more intelligent path choices when traffic must be redirected around a failed router or network.

OSPF is an Internet standard defined by RFC 1583.

Internet Group Membership Protocol (IGMP)

Windows 2000 Server supports version 2 of IGMP as defined in RFC 1112. IGMP, often called IP multicasting, is an Internet standard protocol that allows a single packet to be delivered to multiple hosts. Further, it shifts part of the responsibility for identifying those hosts from the server to the network. Using IGMP, a server can transmit a real-time data stream, such as a video presentation, to any number of subscribers on the network—while transmitting only a single copy of the data. While IGMP is gaining wider acceptance, it is still usable only on the part of the Internet called the multicast backbone (MBONE). The MBONE is a special part of the Internet that is multicast compatible.

Multicasting is similar to broadcasting because both multicast and broadcast packets can be received by multiple hosts. However, broadcast packets interrupt every system on the network, while multicast packets only interrupt those systems that listen for specific multicast IP addresses. Further, broadcasts are generally limited to a single network segment. When used with IGMP, multicast packets can traverse large, routed networks. Multicast packets make use of a special range of IP addresses called Class D addresses, which have a first octet between 224 and 239.

Windows 2000 Server includes an IGMP router and an IGMP proxy. Using these two services, a Windows 2000 Server connected to the MBONE can receive and forward multicast packets on behalf of an intranet. Do not confuse the IGMP router capability with an IGMP routing protocol—Windows 2000 Server is currently not capable of acting as an IGMP router in multirouter environments. IGMP router and proxy settings can be configured from within the Routing And Remote Access snap-in by opening the IGMP Properties dialog box, shown in Figure 6-12.

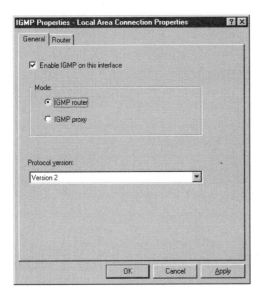

Figure 6-12.
Enabling IGMP is done from the Routing And Remote Access MMC snap-in.

DHCP (Dynamic Host Configuration Protocol) Relay Agent

Windows 2000 Server continues to provide DHCP relay agent functionality. Using the DHCP relay agent, administrators can have all hosts on multiple network segments retrieve their IP address information from a single DHCP server.

Upon startup, a DHCP client transmits a broadcast query requesting an IP address to be used. If a DHCP server is on the same network segment, it will respond with an IP address and any additional information the administrator has configured. However, broadcast queries do not normally pass through routers, so Microsoft provides the DHCP relay agent. By placing a computer with the DHCP relay agent installed on every network segment in a network, DHCP clients do not need to be on the same network segment as the DCHP server. The DHCP relay agent will listen for DHCP requests and forward them to the DHCP server.

To configure the DHCP relay agent in Windows 2000 Server, add the service as a routing protocol using the Routing And Remote Access interface.

Quality of Service (QoS)

If you have ever experienced choppy audio and video across a network, you will appreciate QoS. Windows 2000 uses QoS to prioritize network traffic and make the most efficient use of bandwidth. Further, the QoS features built in to Windows 2000 allow it to request and reserve bandwidth from network hardware.

Real-time applications will see the greatest benefit from the use of QoS. Audio and video streams do not have the opportunity to retransmit packets that are dropped, and they deserve a higher priority than a file transfer that occurs in the background and is not time-sensitive. Applications written specifically to take advantage of the QoS API can benefit by specifying requirements on a per-session basis. For example, Microsoft Windows 2000 Server Media Services can request from the network a specific amount of bandwidth for a given data stream.

Administrators can use the QoS features built in to Windows 2000 Server to give specific users priority on the network, prioritize different types of traffic, guarantee that specific applications receive a dedicated amount of bandwidth, and prevent protocols that don't support QoS (such as UDP) from stealing too many resources. QoS is a complex topic. To work correctly, every piece of equipment on a network must support the same QoS standards. Windows 2000 adds QoS support, but that is only a small part of what is required. Even if the switches and routers on your corporate network support QoS, that will not be sufficient to use QoS across the Internet—your ISP and all ISPs between you and the destination computer must support the standards. Even if this is not the case currently, you can still benefit from using QoS.

To understand QoS, it is important to understand latency and jitter. *Latency* is a measure of delay on a network. Routers are the biggest cause of latency— each router takes a small amount of time to process a packet and forward it to the next network. While an individual router might not add an appreciable amount of latency, the combined latency of all the routers between a client and a server can be significant. In general, the busier a router is, the more latency it adds. Latency is not a problem for real-time audio and video presentations if they are one-way communications (each packet is delayed the same amount and received in appropriate intervals). However, latency presents a serious problem if the communication is two-way, as is the case with Internet telephony and video conferencing. Video conferencing across a high-latency network leads to unnatural pauses that can be frustrating to the participants.

Jitter is the measurement of change in latency. For example, if the average latency of a packet traveling between a client and server is one-half of a second, some packets might take as long as a full second to travel, while others take only a quarter of a second. Jitter is not an important consideration for file transfers, but it has a profound impact on real-time network applications such as audio and video. One of the primary causes of high jitter is a feature of IP networks: different packets in a single session can follow different paths through a network. If different paths have different latency, high jitter results. Clients often compensate for jitter by buffering network traffic, thereby increasing overall delay.

Consistent with Microsoft's goal of making Windows more extensible, Windows 2000 Server provides several APIs to allow third-party software vendors to develop their own QoS standards. There are several QoS standards supported by Windows 2000 Server.

Resource Reservation Setup Protocol (RSVP)

When you place a telephone call, you are never concerned that the quality of your telephone call is going to degrade because your provider becomes busy. Telephone service providers never get that busy; once their network has reached capacity, new telephone calls are rejected completely. Each telephone call that you place is guaranteed a high-quality connection until you hang up your telephone.

This is certainly not the case with most IP networks. If you have ever tried to carry on an audio conversation across a busy IP network, you know that the sound might break up when other network applications steal your bandwidth. Windows 2000 adds the IETF RSVP to provide QoS. RSVP is one method of making IP networks perform more like telephone networks. RSVP allows a system to reserve a predetermined amount of bandwidth along a specific path in the network—eliminating the possibility of bandwidth starvation and reducing jitter. The specific path, combined with the QoS specifications, is called a *flow*.

To reserve a flow, the client and server must have resources allocated from every piece of network hardware that will participate. The client starts the reservation process by sending a *PATH* message to the receiver. As each piece of network hardware receives the PATH message, it adds itself to the list and forwards the message on. This list allows future packets in the same session to follow the same route. Any piece of hardware that does not speak RSVP will forward the message on like any other packet, without adding itself to the list of hardware.

The receiving station then sends a response to the PATH message called an *RESV* (for reservation) message. The RESV message is guaranteed to travel the same route as the PATH message, because each hop in the path is listed in the message. As each piece of hardware forwards the RESV message toward the client, it verifies that it really does have the requested bandwidth and actually reserves it. The entire RSVP reservation process is illustrated in Figure 6-13. If one of the pieces of hardware cannot reserve the resources, an error message indicates the problem. The jitter that can occur by using varying paths is reduced because all packets in that session will pass through exactly the same routers.

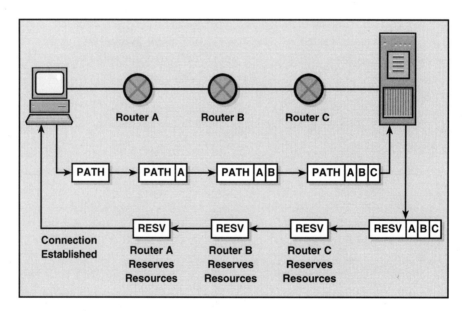

Figure 6-13.
Both a PATH and an RESV message are required to reserve resources using RSVP.

The sender automatically resends a PATH message on a regular basis to adapt to changing states in the network. By default, this resend of the PATH message occurs every 30 seconds. If the network hardware that has reserved resources does not see a PATH message within a certain amount of time (defaulting to 90 seconds), it will remove the reservation. This prevents a failed connection from tying up resources unnecessarily. When the session is complete, the station that breaks the connection will send a special PATH message instructing the network hardware to release the resources. This is called a *PATH-tear* message.

Traffic Control

Traffic control is analogous to assigning priorities to different processes within the operating system—the most important processes receive the most processor time, and therefore become more responsive to the user. The traffic control API provides the operating system with finer control over the packets it generates, allowing it to make better use of network bandwidth.

Traffic control and RSVP are not mutually exclusive. On the contrary, they complement each other well. Traffic control can be used across parts of the network that do not support RSVP. In fact, RSVP and traffic control can be used together on a single session where only some of the network components support RSVP.

Packet Scheduling

Not all network traffic is created equal. If you are uploading a large file via File Transfer Protocol (FTP), it would be nice if this transfer would not hurt the performance of the Telnet session you have open. In this scenario, you are not concerned about the time the FTP transfer takes, but you do want Telnet to be more responsive. The operating system should be able to prioritize your Telnet packets so that they are sent before FTP packets.

The QoS Packet Scheduler does just this. It retrieves packets from the outgoing queue and transmits them according to QoS parameters. These parameters allow users and applications to specify that certain applications have a higher priority in the packet queue. If congestion exists, higher priority packets will be bumped to the front of the queue, reducing for these packets latency caused by the local network segment.

External Prioritization (Diff-Serv, 802.1p, and IP Precedence)

IETF Diff-Serv is an IETF working group whose mission is to make use of the 6-bit Type Of Service field included in the IP header. The Type Of Service field was included to be used by network hardware to prioritize packets, but it was never implemented. Windows 2000 Server now allows applications to set priority, allowing this field to specify a level of QoS when compatible network hardware is used.

QoS extends to layer 2 of the OSI model for Ethernet networks. Windows 2000 supports the IEEE 802.1p priority standard to allow switches to prioritize frames. The priority is carried as a 2-byte tag in the data portion of the frame. This allows switches to drop low-priority frames when their queue is full, increasing the chance for high-priority frames to be carried successfully on a busy network segment.

The OSI Model

Computers communicate on networks by agreeing on standard languages, also known as protocols. Each network communication relies on several protocols. To make it even more confusing, protocols are hierarchical—they rely on one another. Fortunately, there's a standard way of organizing them—the OSI model. The OSI model consists of seven distinct layers, and all network protocols exist at one of these seven layers:

- **Application layer (layer 7).** This highest level is used directly by applications to communicate on a network. Examples of protocols at this layer are HTTP, SMTP, and FTP.

- **Presentation layer (layer 6).** Rarely used. It is intended to act as an interface between the session layer and the application layer.

- **Session layer (layer 5).** Provides complex conversation controls. NetBIOS over TCP/IP is the best example of a session layer protocol.

- **Transport layer (layer 4).** Allows for connection-oriented communications, error-checking, and guaranteed delivery. TCP and UDP are the most common examples.

- **Network layer (layer 3).** Provides for routing, navigation, and addressing. IP and IPX are the most popular examples.

- **Data link layer (layer 2).** Provides communications within a single network segment. Protocols can include collision avoidance and error checking. Ethernet, token ring, and FDDI (Fiber Distributed Data Interface) are all layer 2 protocols.

- **Physical layer (layer 1).** The format of the cables and electrical signals. Cat 5 copper wire, fiber optics, and repeaters live at this level.

At layer 3 of the OSI model, IP Precedence allows routers to prioritize traffic and to better select packets that must be dropped. IP Precedence is simpler than the RSVP protocol because it does not require the PATH and RECV messages, nor does it require network hardware to preallocate the necessary resources. However, bandwidth is not guaranteed and jitter is still prevalent.

ISSLOW—Latency Reduction on Slow Links

Using ISSLOW, large packets can be fragmented to improve performance. Consider the example of audio and video being transmitted simultaneously. Video packets are much larger than audio packets, and the delay while the packet is transmitted over a slow link can be as much as half a second. If audio packets are separated by half-second intervals, the quality of the audio becomes unacceptable.

ISSLOW solves this problem by fragmenting large packets into multiple, smaller packets. This way, many smaller audio packets can be transmitted in the middle of the big packets, ensuring a smooth service quality. ISSLOW is the name of an IETF working group—the actual letters represent "ISSLL subgroup on low bitrate links."

Quality of Service Admission Control Service (QoS ACS)

The Quality of Service Admission Control Service (QoS ACS) allows administrators to control which users and groups can reserve bandwidth on the network. Naturally, RSVP could be dangerous if control wasn't provided—a user could request so much bandwidth that the rest of the organization suffered! QoS ACS uses policies to determine whether resource requests should be approved or disapproved. QoS ACS controls RSVP, SBM (Subnet Bandwidth Management), IP Precedence, and 802.1p usage to prevent bandwidth overcommitment on both routers and network segments.

QoS ACS policies can be based on network topology, available resources, users, groups, and applications. These policies are stored in Active Directory, so they are available across the enterprise. QoS ACS is an open standard, so third-party switches and routers can make use of Windows 2000 Active Directory to determine policy.

How Do Other Operating Systems Fit In?

Windows 2000 Server is intended to provide network services to a variety of clients, including Windows for Workgroups, Windows 95, Windows 98, Windows 2000 Professional, and UNIX operating systems. More recent versions of the

Windows operating systems will benefit the most from the network advances added to Windows 2000 Server. For example, Windows 98 systems are shipped ready to participate in Active Directories and to use Microsoft Distributed file system (Dfs) shares.

Summary

As the Internet continues to evolve, so does Windows. The new networking features of Windows 2000 Server enable administrators to take better advantage of their existing network and of the Internet. Virtual private networking technologies like PPTP, L2TP, and IPSec improve security and increase the usefulness of the Internet. The routing features of Windows 2000 Server expand the operating system's functionality past that of merely a file and application server. Finally, system-level support for Quality of Service technologies makes real-time multimedia over IP networks a reality. Ultimately, all these technological advancements lead to more productive and happier users.

CHAPTER SEVEN

Communications

Overview

The greatest modern achievements of computing depend on the network, and this situation will certainly continue. Today, Microsoft Windows 2000 Server runs alongside and often has replaced certain network hardware, telephone switches, videoconferencing equipment, and even the telephone.

Routing And Remote Access allows users to connect over ordinary phone lines to a corporate network. It can also allow Internet service provider (ISP) customers access to the Internet. Most importantly, it can provide these services in an extremely secure, efficient, scalable, and flexible manner.

The Telephony API helps developers integrate Windows 2000 Server into voice networks. Though the technologies are still being developed, administrators who install Windows networks now are prepared to take advantage of IP telephony by simply adding the software.

Audio and video conferencing is a built-in feature of Windows 2000 Server. Windows Media Services are shipped with the operating system, allowing anyone who purchases the software to take advantage of the advanced streaming media technologies.

This chapter introduces these technologies. After reading the chapter, you will have a good understanding of which technologies will benefit your organization.

Routing And Remote Access

The Routing And Remote Access feature of Windows 2000 allows systems to network over ordinary phone lines. It has also been called Remote Access Service (RAS) and Dial-Up Networking, and it has existed in one form or another within every version of Windows NT. Typically, Windows 95, Windows 98, and Windows NT Workstation systems act as remote access clients and Windows NT Servers act as remote access servers.

Windows 2000 Professional continues to support both client-side and server-side remote access communications. A variety of connection types are supported:

- Analog phone lines with modems
- ISDN lines
- X.25 lines
- Null modem cables

Clients and servers can securely connect and transparently perform any network task using any of these connection types. Today, the most common use of remote access is to connect to an ISP using an analog phone line and a 56k modem.

Windows 2000 Server expands upon the traditional remote access capabilities by allowing clients on an internal network to communicate through the Internet. It can also leverage the dial-up connection to create a virtual private network (VPN) so that all network communications are private and secure. These new features mean that Windows 2000 Servers will be used as remote access clients more often, because they will share a dial-up connection with the rest of the network. For more information on remote access as a router, please refer to Chapter 6, "Network Infrastructure."

The Routing And Remote Access feature included with Windows 2000 Server has many features beyond allowing clients to dial in and gain access to an internal network. This new feature is integrated into Active Directory, so you can control whether a user is allowed to dial in by editing that user's properties. This is an improvement over previous versions of Windows that required administrators to use a separate tool.

Administrators now have greater control over MPPP (Multilink Point-to-Point Protocol). The Bandwidth Allocation Protocol (BAP) gives administrators the ability to specify the circumstances in which multiple links will be used simultaneously. Telephone company charges can be reduced by setting specific criteria for the addition and deletion of additional links—yet another way that Windows 2000 Server helps reduce an organization's total cost of ownership.

Macintosh dial-in clients are now supported using their native AppleTalk Remote Access Protocol (ARAP). This feature is new to the Windows family of operating systems. Of course, Macintosh clients can continue to connect using PPP (Point-to-Point Protocol).

Remote access is administered through the Routing And Remote Access MMC snap-in tool available from the Administrative Tools program group on the Start menu.

Extensible Authentication Protocol (EAP)

The Extensible Authentication Protocol (EAP) allows for new ways for remote access users to be validated. The most significant improvement over previous versions of Windows will allow software developers to provide other means of authentication beyond those included with the operating system. However, Microsoft has provided several EAP authentication methods that can be used without needing any development. Out of the box, Windows 2000 supports Message Digest 5 Challenge Handshake Authentication Protocol (EAP-MD5 CHAP), Transport Level Security (EAP-TLS), and Remote Authentication Dial-In User Service (EAP-RADIUS).

Smart cards that provide one-time password authentication are becoming common in corporate networks that demand high levels of security. EAP will allow Windows 2000 to take advantage of the new technologies. EAP-TLS is the strongest of the different authentication methods and is the correct type for use with smart cards.

Many organizations rely on separate RADIUS servers to provide authentication for all servers on the network. This is particularly common in multiplatform networks, because RADIUS can be used by NetWare, UNIX, and Windows servers. The EAP-RADIUS component will pass remote access authentication requests to a specified RADIUS server on the network, allowing remote access clients to be authenticated by the same method used on the internal network.

EAP is enabled using the Routing And Remote Access utility. Simply view the properties of the server, select the Security tab, and select the Extensible Authentication Protocol (EAP) check box, as shown in Figure 7-1 on the following page.

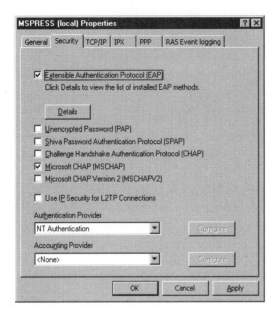

Figure 7-1.
Enabling EAP authentication is done through the Routing And Remote Access utility.

EAP is defined by RFC 2284. EAP-TLS and EAP-RADIUS are currently in the draft stages.

Remote Access Policies

Remote Access Policies allow tight control over who can make a remote access connection, how that person can be authenticated, and when he or she is allowed to connect. Remote Access Policies also leverage Active Directory. As such, they can be easily applied to remote access servers within an entire organization. Administrators of small networks might not need to configure policies, but they are crucial to the efficient operation of remote access in larger networks.

The new support for Remote Access Policies improves network security. One way that administrators can reduce the opportunity for attackers to gain access to the network through remote access is by narrowing the time window for users to dial in. For example, if a particular user only dials in between 8:00 AM and 5:00 PM on the weekends, a policy can be created so that the user account will be refused a connection during any other time. This is configured by using a simple graphical interface, as shown in Figure 7-2.

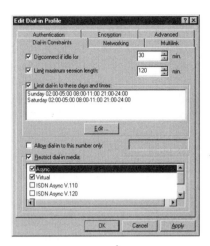

Figure 7-2.
Remote Access Policies allow for specific dial-in constraints.

Policies can also be used to reduce costs. Administrators can reduce the number of active but idle remote access links by creating a policy that limits the session time for specific users and groups. Administrators can also limit the number of lines involved in MPPP connections by creating a BAP policy. Figure 7-3 shows how an administrator can configure the MPPP and BAP options.

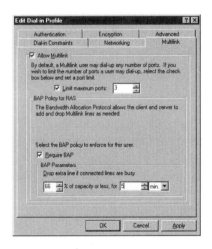

Figure 7-3.
Save money through restricting bandwidth use by dial-in users.

Overall, eleven different properties can be used to create a policy. These include

- Remote access client and server IP addresses
- Remote access client and server phone numbers
- Connection type
- Time of day
- User groups
- Remote access client computer name

To configure Remote Access Policies, start by launching the Routing And Remote Access MMC snap-in. Right-click on the server you wish to configure policies for, and select Remote Access Policies.

Telephony Application Programming Interface (TAPI)

IP telephony is a technology that will merge data and voice networks. In most modern organizations, two separate networks are maintained:

- A voice network that utilizes a private branch exchange (PBX) and facilitates forwarding calls, voice mail, conference calls, and other traditional business phone functions
- A data network that allows computers to connect for sharing data, exchanging e-mail, and performing video conferencing

Merging these two networks can make an organization more efficient in several ways. First, most large organizations have separate staffs to maintain each of these two networks. If the two networks could be merged, fewer administrators would be required. Second, separate wiring and equipment is required for each network. Merging the two would reduce the cost of starting a business *and* reduce the costs associated with maintaining the hardware. Finally, computers are far more powerful and flexible tools than telephones. When you allow a computer to handle the transfer of voice data, many advanced features are possible. This is illustrated in Figure 7-4.

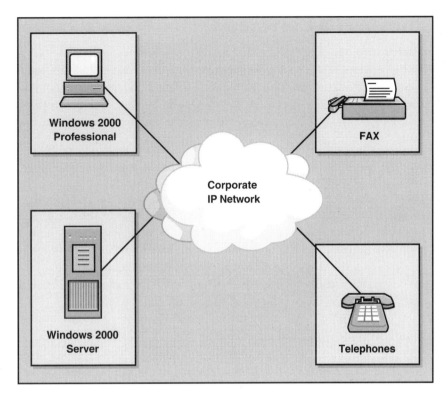

Figure 7-4.
TAPI 3.0 gives developers a platform for IP telephony.

Windows 2000 Server is the first Microsoft operating system to provide support for TAPI 3.0. The Telephony Application Programming Interface (TAPI) provides a way for applications to use the telephony functionality built in to the operating system. Microsoft is providing only the framework for software developers—software does not ship with the operating system that will allow Windows 2000 Server to perform IP telephony. However, by providing a uniform set of interfaces for developers, Microsoft is ensuring that Windows is ready to participate in IP telephony when the technology matures.

TAPI 3.0 takes advantage of several advanced technologies. Because it is implemented using the Component Object Model (COM), developers can use any development environment of their choosing. TAPI's integration into Active Directory will allow administrators to easily manage TAPI services throughout the enterprise. Finally, TAPI takes advantage of the Quality of Service capabilities described in Chapter Six, "Network Infrastructure."

Windows Media Services

Microsoft Windows Media Services (formerly known as NetShow) is included with Windows 2000 Server. In the past, Windows Media Services was available as an entirely separate application. Microsoft has chosen to include it as part of the operating system to provide Windows administrators with streaming media server capabilities. This section will describe the features of Windows Media Services, but covering the component in detail is outside the scope of this book.

What Windows Media Services Provides

Windows Media Services provides streaming media services across intranets and the Internet. *Streaming media* is a generic term for real-time audio and video viewing and conferencing.

Users on a corporate network can use Windows Media Services to video-conference with other employees without relying on independent hardware. They can also record audio or video presentations for later playback. When used this way, Windows Media Services becomes an excellent tool for employee training.

Organizations that host web sites will also find many uses for Windows Media Services. Use of the tool on the Internet is different than on intranets, because bandwidth on the Internet is much less available and latency tends to be much higher. Audio and video conferencing is still possible, but at a lower quality than is possible across an intranet. One use of Windows Media Services on the Internet is to make presentations and press releases available to customers after those events have occurred.

Along with Windows Media Services, Windows 2000 Server provides tools to help author Advanced Streaming Format (ASF) files. ASF files contain the data that the Windows Media Services server uses to create its streaming media. For more information on the tools available, please refer to the Windows Media Services online documentation in Windows 2000 Server.

What About the Clients?

Clients must have special software to use Windows Media Services streams. Fortunately, the Windows Media Player software is freely available from Microsoft's Web site at

```
http://www.microsoft.com/windows/mediaplayer/download/
```

How to Install and Administer Windows Media Services

When you installed Windows 2000 Server, it automatically added a shortcut (in the Windows Media Services group of your Programs menu) to launch the Windows Media Services setup routine. This shortcut launches the setup wizard, which guides you through the installation of the Windows Media Services server.

After it is installed, Windows Media Services is administered using an HTML interface, as pictured in Figure 7-5. The HTML interface allows Windows Media Services to be administered from any system that supports Microsoft Internet Explorer and DCOM.

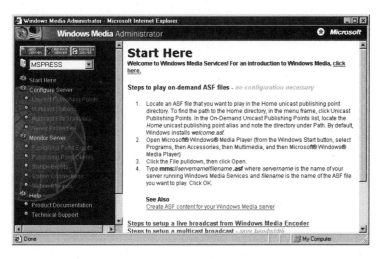

Figure 7-5.
Windows Media Services is administered using Internet Explorer.

How Windows Media Services Works

The Windows Media Services server provides several ways to send data to clients. Supporting a variety of technologies allows more advanced clients to benefit from the improved performance of the newest protocols, while still allowing legacy software and hardware to participate. Additionally, users protected by a firewall can choose from several protocols to find one that is acceptable to their network security. For specific information about the protocols available, please refer to the Windows Media Services online documentation in Windows 2000 Server.

Summary

Routing And Remote Access, Telephony Application Programming Interface, and Windows Media Services provide advanced communications capabilities to Windows-based networks. The newest versions of each of these components are included in Windows 2000 Server, adding many features not found in previous generations of the software.

Administrators can take advantage of greater control over dial-in use by implementing remote access policies. The Extensible Authentication Protocol improves the security of dial-up networks and, more important, allows for different methods of verifying a user's identity. Windows networks are ready to participate in IP telephony, thanks to the inclusion of TAPI 3.0. Finally, Windows Media Services brings native audio and video streaming capabilities to Windows 2000 Server.

CHAPTER EIGHT

Internet Information Services

Overview

Internet Information Services (IIS) has been the core of Microsoft's web services since the first version was released for Windows NT 3.51. IIS is one of the fastest evolving applications ever; each successive generation of the software shows major improvements in flexibility, performance, and stability. Microsoft Windows 2000 Server ships with version 5 of IIS. The new features increase the stability and security of web servers. Web hosting environments that place multiple customers on a single machine will benefit the most.

IIS is a massive product that cannot be documented within this book. Instead, this chapter will introduce you to the new features in IIS 5.0. This chapter assumes you have a general knowledge of previous versions of IIS.

New Wizards

IIS 5.0 features additional wizards targeted specifically to the most difficult tasks in IIS 4.0. The Certificate Wizard can be used instead of Key Manager to create Secure Sockets Layer (SSL) certificates. The Permissions Wizard provides a simple way of modifying access control lists on files. Together, these wizards will make IIS available to a wider audience and reduce the number of problems users experience.

Certificate Wizard

Many users of previous versions of IIS experienced problems using the Key Manager utility, or keyring. As shown in Figure 8-1 on the following page, the new Certificate Wizard replaces keyring with a simple, quick interface. This new GUI provides greater flexibility, too, allowing the administrator to request certificates from Certification Authorities, such as Verisign, *and* to request certificates from Certificate Services that might be running on the local network.

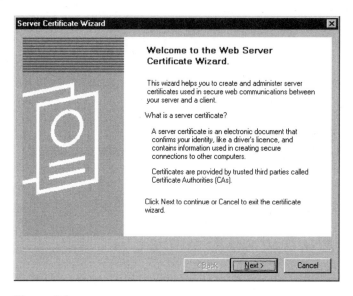

Figure 8-1.
The Certificate Wizard replaces Key Manager.

Now organizations can create SSL certificates in a much shorter time frame than before. If you are your own Certification Authority and you have administrative rights on your network, Hypertext Transfer Protocols (HTTPs) can be set up on a web server in just a few minutes. Figure 8-2 shows the Certificate Wizard being directed to request a certificate from a Certificate server on the network—a simple process indeed. This wizard is also capable of importing certificates that were created with Key Manager and previous versions of IIS.

Permissions Wizard

The Permissions Wizard, as shown in Figure 8-3, will save webmasters time by reducing the complexity of assigning file permissions. In the past, file permissions were the source of many problems. Permissions that were too restrictive would cause content to be displayed incorrectly. Often, web content was not restricted at all, creating a security risk. These problems are solved by the Permissions Wizard.

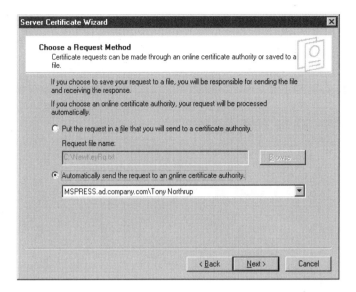

Figure 8-2.
The Certificate Wizard can automatically request a new certificate from a Windows 2000 Certificate Service.

Figure 8-3.
The Permissions Wizard will make it easier to manage web sites.

You no longer need to understand how NTFS file permissions relate to IIS security to maintain a secure web site. The Permissions Wizard will analyze your directory structure and provide a recommendation for security settings. Figure 8-4 shows the wizard's accurate recommendations for a virtual directory. Alternatively, you can use templates to configure the security to your specifications.

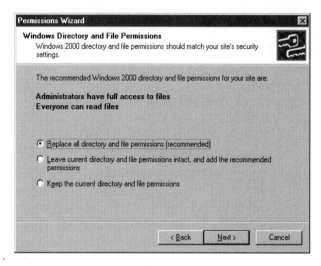

Figure 8-4.
The Permissions Wizard will recommend security settings for virtual directories.

Process Accounting

As discussed in Chapter 1, changes within the Windows 2000 kernel allow individual processes to be tightly controlled. As a result, webmasters can monitor and limit the processor time individual virtual servers consume. The graphical user interface of the Internet Information Services snap-in enables this.

To monitor the processor time consumed by individual web requests, start by viewing the properties of the web site. Edit the logging properties of the virtual web. Select the Extended Properties tab, and select the Process Accounting check box as shown in Figure 8-5. After these changes are applied, all web requests will include information about the processor. This information can be used in reports to determine which pages and which virtual webs consume the most resources.

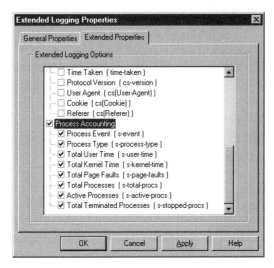

Figure 8-5.
Use Extended Logging Properties for process accounting.

Web hosting services will be able to bill customers of shared web servers based on the processor time their pages consume. This is particularly useful in environments where Active Server Pages are common. Developers will also find the process accounting feature useful when optimizing their code.

Processor Throttling

Administrators can now guarantee that no single virtual web server consumes more than its fair share of processor time. By editing the properties of a virtual web, as shown in Figure 8-6 on the following page, the webmaster can direct IIS to add an event to the event log each time a virtual web exceeds a percentage of the CPU's time. By selecting the Enforce Limits check box, IIS will restrict the virtual server from executing until other processes have had their turn.

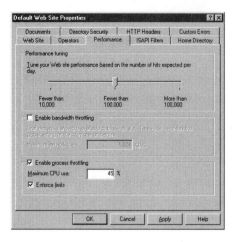

Figure 8-6.
Processor throttling enables administrators to restrict a virtual server's allotment of CPU cycles.

HTTP Compression

A great deal of the bandwidth on the Internet is consumed by transmitting HTML (Hypertext Markup Language) files. While HTML documents tend to be much smaller than images and streaming media, they are the most commonly requested type of file. They are simply text files that contain special codes that web browsers interpret to format the text.

Text files are extremely compressible. In most cases, the size of large HTML files can be reduced by more than 80 percent. Therefore, it makes sense in most cases that large HTML files should be compressed before they are transmitted onto the network. Before IIS 5.0, compression of text files before transmission was not common.

IIS 5.0 allows HTTP compression to be enabled. HTTP compression can be used to compress any type of file, but HTML files will exhibit the greatest benefit. The benefit of HTTP compression isn't as great with image files, perhaps the largest consumer of bandwidth, because image files are generally compressed in their native format.

To turn on HTTP compression, open the Internet Information Services MMC snap-in and view the server properties. Edit the Master Properties of the WWW Service. Select the Service tab, and check either or both the Compress Application Files option and the Compress Static Files option. A sample configuration is shown in Figure 8-7.

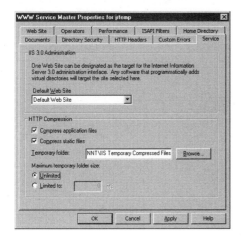

Figure 8-7.
HTTP compression can reduce the bandwidth used by IIS.

This new feature reduces the bandwidth used by IIS but increases the load on the server's processors. Compression requires additional processing time, so you should not enable this feature on a system that will be bottlenecked by increased processor usage. Whenever you turn on compression, monitor the server to verify that performance has been helped, not hurt.

NOTE: Both the client and the server must support HTTP compression for it to be used. Currently Microsoft Internet Explorer versions 4 and 5 and Netscape Navigator 4 support it.

Compressing static files places less demand on the server than compressing application files does. Static files can be compressed once—a cached copy of the compressed file can then be used until the file is modified. However, application files such as Perl scripts and Active Server Pages might change every time they are transmitted. Therefore, the server must recompress them each time they are sent. Enabling compression of static files has little negative impact on the performance of the server's CPUs. Compressing application files has a much more profound impact.

This HTTP extension is still in its infancy, but preliminary studies show an overall performance improvement of 30 percent for users with a 28.8 Kbps modem.

Active Server Pages (ASP)

Active Server Pages (ASP) is a technology that enables IIS to process a script and send the output of that script as an HTML file. Several new features have been added to ASP for IIS 5.0. Developers can create ASP code that is more efficient and returns articulate error messages. Overall ASP performance has been improved. ASP will now tune itself to avoid being blocked by a single process. Previously this tuning was a manual process. ASP files that do not contain ASP script code will be processed as HTML files, allowing developers to create all documents with the extension .asp without suffering performance degradation.

Distributed Authoring and Versioning (DAV)

Distributed Authoring and Versioning (DAV) extends HTTP/1.1 to allow greater authoring capabilities using a standard protocol. Several applications, such as Microsoft FrontPage and Netscape Composer, currently allow files on a web server to be modified. DAV seeks to allow such authoring tools more robust control over the files on a web server. The ultimate goal is to allow HTTP to be used as a file-sharing protocol.

HTTP with DAV extensions can be used to

- Add, remove, and change files and folders

- Rename, copy, and move files and folders

- Search for directories and files

- Lock files to keep other users from editing them simultaneously

- Change access control lists

- Download the file source (for example, download an ASP file without processing it)

HTTP with DAV extensions is a standard Internet protocol currently being developed by the IETF (Internet Engineering Task Force) working group named webdav. To make use of the protocol, you will need an editing application that uses the DAV extensions to HTTP/1.1. As these client applications become available, IIS 5.0 will be ready to support them.

NOTE: For more information on webdav, visit *http://ietf.org/ html.charters/webdav-charter.html.*

Digest Authentication

Digest authentication is a feature of HTTP/1.1 that improves upon basic authentication. Digest authentication hashes the password information before it is transmitted, ensuring that nobody can intercept and decrypt the password. Session-specific and time-specific information is added to the hash, removing any possibility that the password could be retransmitted in its hashed format. Digest authentication provides an alternative to NT LAN Manager (NTLM) Challenge/Response that is more secure than basic authentication.

Server Gated Cryptography (SGC)

SGC, or Server Gated Cryptography, works around the export restrictions on 128-bit encryption. It is intended to allow secure financial transactions using 128 bits, both domestic and internationally. SGC can be used outside the United States because it is limited to specific uses, including online banking. Similar to needing a certificate for SSL encryption, a special SGC certificate is required to use SGC.

Fortezza

This feature was added to IIS specifically to meet the needs of the U.S. government. Fortezza relies on hardware to aid encryption, a requirement of several government agencies. In a nutshell, government employees are assigned a credit-card-like device that has a large token encoded within it. This token can be read by means of a credit card reader and used instead of a password.

Fortezza can be used to

- Keep messages secret
- Validate the content of a message
- Authenticate the sender and receiver of a message
- Restrict access to specific users

Summary

The new features in Internet Information Services are the direct result of feedback from users. The new features make IIS easier to use and make it run more efficiently, securely, and reliably.

The Certificate Wizard replaces the Key Manager utility, making it a simple task to request an SSL certificate. The Permissions Wizard can be used instead of Windows Explorer to assign file permissions. Combined, these features make IIS a viable platform for Web hosting and e-commerce.

HTTP compression reduces bandwidth usage by shrinking HTML files before transmission. Distributed Authoring and Versioning will allow greater flexibility in the way files are shared across intranets and the Internet. The new features built into ASP will make developing Active Server Pages easier than ever. Process accounting and processor throttling allow webmasters to monitor and restrict processor usage with respect to virtual servers and individual pages.

IIS 5.0 has several new security features. Digest Authentication can be used instead of basic authentication to validate users without transmitting any form of their password across the network. Fortezza meets strict government requirements for hardware-based identification information. Server Gated Cryptography allows banks to perform worldwide transactions using 128-bit security.

PART IV

DISTRIBUTED SERVICES

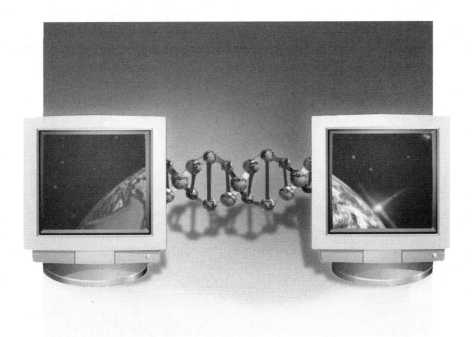

CHAPTER NINE

Overview of Distributed Services

Overview

This chapter covers some of the distributed services included with Microsoft Windows 2000 Server. Distributed services are defined as network services that can span multiple machines. This architecture offers several advantages over nondistributed services:

- If one server fails, clients can use a different server.
- Wide Area Network (WAN) traffic is reduced because servers can be placed strategically throughout the organization.
- Load on each server is reduced because client requests are distributed among multiple servers.

These are good reasons to implement distributed services on your network, but there are drawbacks as well:

- Multiple systems must be administered to provide a single service.
- Increasing the number of servers also increases the chances of failures and the complexity of the problems.
- Traffic between servers increases for data synchronization.
- Delays in synchronization can lead to invalid data being returned to clients.

The following sections will introduce you to the Windows 2000 Server Distributed Services, including DNS (Domain Name System), WINS (Windows Internet Name Service), Active Directory, DHCP (Dynamic Host Configuration Protocol), and the Class Store.

Windows 2000 Namespace

A namespace, when used in the context of networking, is a type of directory. For example, the table of contents of this book forms a namespace in which chapters can be resolved to page numbers. Telephone books provide a namespace for resolving names to telephone numbers. A particular administrator is responsible for maintaining a Windows 2000 namespace.

Windows 2000 networks have three primary distributed namespaces. DNS forms a namespace of IP addresses and host names. WINS manages the namespace of IP addresses and NetBIOS names and can be closely tied to DNS. Active Directory provides a namespace for resolving the names of network objects to the objects themselves. Each of these services is described in more detail in the sections that follow.

DNS (Domain Name System)

The most commonly used namespace on the Internet is DNS, the Domain Name System. DNS forms a namespace between fully qualified domain names (FQDNs) and IP addresses. This allows applications to accept a friendly name like mspress.microsoft.com and resolve it to an IP address. As the Internet grows in popularity, so does DNS. FQDNs are now a common way for companies to identify themselves.

DNS was designed to grow to large scales. It is a distributed, hierarchical, extensible database. Ownership of the database is divided by splitting it into different domains. The common top-level domains (org, net, com, and edu) are owned by an organization called InterNIC. InterNIC is responsible for delegating authority for second-level domains within its top-level domains.

Microsoft owns a second-level domain named Microsoft beneath the top-level domain named com. These domain names are combined and separated by periods to form the domain name microsoft.com. Companies can further subdivide their domains, forming extended names such as mspress.microsoft.com. This convention is shown in Figure 9-1.

NOTE: Find out more about the InterNIC at *www.internic.net*!

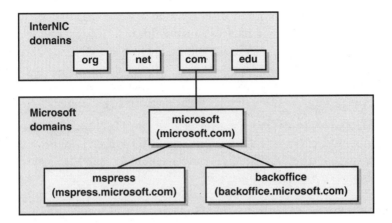

Figure 9-1.
DNS domain structure.

Companies are responsible for creating additional resource records within their domains. There are many different types of resource records stored in a DNS database. The most common type is the A (address) resource record, which maps a host name to an IP address. A common example of a host name on the Internet is www, a name used to identify Web servers. MX (Mail eXchange) records identify mail servers within an organization. WINS records store NetBIOS names and allow integration of WINS and DNS.

DNS servers can become extremely busy on large networks. To reduce the load on any given server, domains can be separated into *zones*. Zones split the responsibility of a domain between multiple servers. To keep the servers in a zone synchronized, servers transfer data between each other using *zone transfers*.

The DNS Query and Lookup Process

Clients make use of the DNS database by performing a DNS lookup. The client will send a packet to the DNS server it has been previously configured with and wait for a response. The DNS server will attempt to find an answer for the client's question—exactly how this happens varies. If the server is responsible, or *authoritative*, for the domain being queried, the server will definitely return an answer. Even if the answer is along the lines of "I can't find a host by that name," an authoritative server will know without any doubt that it has the correct information.

If the server is not authoritative, it might need to pass the query to another DNS server. For example, if a user within the domain mspress.microsoft.com attempts to reach the server www.internic.net, the mspress DNS server will need to forward the query to another server if it hasn't already cached the answer. Ultimately, the query might be forwarded through several servers before it finally reaches the authoritative DNS servers for the internic.net domain.

> NOTE: This is a *very* brief overview of the DNS query process. For more information, refer to Windows 2000 Server's online documentation or the DNS FAQ at *www.microsoft.com/ntserver/nts/ deployment/planguide/dnswp.asp.*

Host Names and Computer Names

Host names in DNS are different from computer names that are assigned to Windows systems. Computer names are used in NetBIOS naming. WINS manages the NetBIOS namespace. You will find more information on WINS later in this chapter. It is a very good idea to make computer names and host names correspond, but it is not a requirement.

Host names are commonly composed of lowercase letters, numbers, and hyphens. This is more restrictive than NetBIOS names, which also allow the use of underscores and periods. However, NetBIOS names are limited to 15 characters, significantly less than the 24-character length of host names. For best results on networks that use both DNS and NetBIOS, assign all computers case-insensitive names of 15 characters or less that have no special characters.

DNS Dynamic Update Protocol

One of the most significant disadvantages to traditional DNS is its static nature. Administrators manage the DNS database, and changes to IP addresses are manually entered. A more automated solution would allow servers to communicate their IP addresses directly to the DNS server, eliminating the manual intervention of the administrator.

The DNS dynamic update protocol allows this automation to happen. This extension to traditional DNS allows hosts on the network to send a special message to a domain's primary DNS server that will result in a change to the database. The implications are significant:

■ DHCP servers can update DNS to ensure that the same host name identifies a roving computer.

- Active Directory servers can insert themselves into the DNS database automatically.

- WINS servers can register NetBIOS names into any dynamic update database.

The DNS services built into Windows 2000 Server support DNS dynamic update protocol, and using those services will give you the best results when working with Active Directory. However, other DNS servers support dynamic update as well, including UNIX-based DNS servers. Ask the software vendor to verify that a particular software supports RFC 2136.

WINS (Windows Internet Name Service)

WINS (Windows Internet Name Service) has been a standard component of Windows TCP/IP networking for several generations. The network protocol is an Internet standard defined in RFC 1001 and RFC 1002. WINS is responsible for the entire NetBIOS namespace on a network, including registrations for every desktop, server, domain controller, and the NetBIOS services running on each machine.

WINS allows information to be registered and retrieved. For example, when a server starts up, it registers each of its NetBIOS names and the associated IP addresses with the configured WINS server. Later, clients are able to find the server's IP address by querying the WINS server with the NetBIOS name. This process is illustrated in Figure 9-2 on the next page.

NetBIOS names are 16-byte identifiers that specify both a service and a system (or group of systems) on a network. For example, a computer named MONTY with the Workstation service running would register the NetBIOS name MONTY..........[00]. The first 15 bytes are used for the computer name (padded with null bytes), and the sixteenth byte identifies the service.

Many staples of Windows networking rely on NetBIOS naming to find servers on the network. Print servers, file servers, messaging services, alert services, and domain controllers all must be able to resolve a NetBIOS name to connect to a remote server. WINS servers provide a directory to allow systems to find each other.

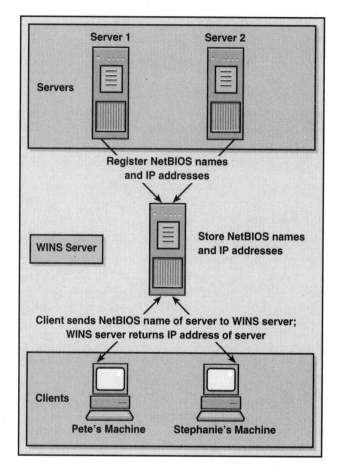

Figure 9-2.
WINS provides a NetBIOS name to the IP address directory.

Windows 2000 no longer depends on NetBIOS for TCP/IP networking. However, you might not be done with WINS! WINS will still be required to support older Microsoft clients, so you will need to continue to maintain it until all computers on the network have been upgraded to Windows 2000. Fortunately, Windows 2000 Server provides a WINS service for backward compatibility.

New WINS Features

The WINS utility has been improved to operate as a Microsoft Management Console (MMC) snap-in, as shown in Figure 9-3. This new interface provides a more powerful searching capability that administrators of large networks will find useful. It also includes utilities to confirm the consistency of records between different WINS servers, automating the process of verifying whether a particular record has been replicated. The database itself can be exported into comma-delimited format, making it more accessible from other applications.

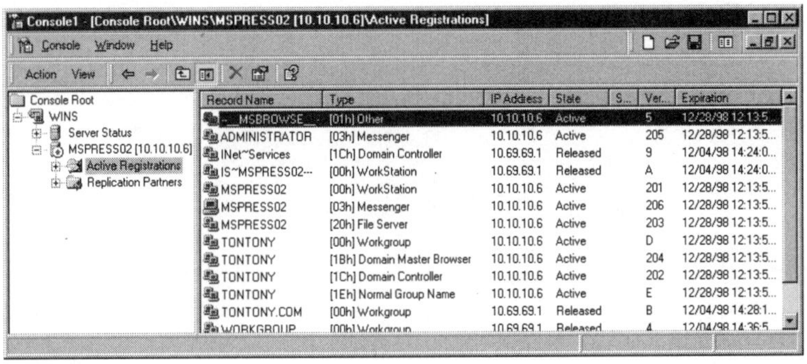

Figure 9-3.
The new WINS utility is an MMC snap-in.

WINS itself has many new features, making it desirable to upgrade existing Microsoft Windows NT 4.0–based WINS servers. Records can now be tombstoned manually, making it easier for administrators to remove names from a large set of WINS servers. Connections established to replicate WINS records can now be kept open, reducing the overhead of establishing a new connection every time records are exchanged. Persistent connections also reduce the time to convergence—how long it takes for changes to replicate to all WINS servers.

The WINS client software, which handles registering and looking up names with a remote WINS server, has also been improved. Now as many as 12 separate WINS servers can be named. This is an improvement over previous versions of Windows that allowed clients to select from only two WINS servers. Additionally, client systems do not need to reboot to renew the registration of their local NetBIOS names.

WINS Architecture

The WINS architecture has not changed from previous versions of Windows. It is similar to the new Active Directory in many ways: multiple servers provide redundancy for each other, and any server can read or write to the database. WINS configuration is much more laborious than Active Directory configuration. Push and pull replication relationships can be created to define how data is sent through the network, but it is a manual process that often requires complicated tuning.

127

A WINS server with several replication partners configured is shown in Figure 9-4. A more automated process also exists, called automatic partner configuration, but it relies on multicast traffic to configure the replication and so will not work in most environments. WINS automatic partner configuration is most useful in single subnet networks with three or fewer WINS servers.

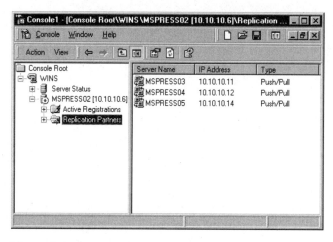

Figure 9-4.
WINS allows push and pull replication relationships to be configured between servers.

DNS and WINS Integration

As with previous versions of Windows NT, DNS and WINS are integrated. DNS can be configured to check a WINS database for the existence of a host name that it cannot find within DNS. (One of the settings for this configuration is illustrated in Figure 9-5.) For example, suppose the computer MSPRESS01 has registered with a WINS server but does not have a DNS entry. Users on the network can resolve the name mspress01.mspress.microsoft.com to its IP address, because the DNS server will query the WINS server and return an answer to the client. This feature is useful in environments with older versions of Windows.

Migrating Away from WINS

As I mentioned earlier, not everyone is ready for life without WINS. If your network has DOS, Windows for Workgroups, Windows 95, Windows 98, Windows NT, or UNIX-based clients using SAMBA, you will need to maintain a

WINS server on your network. If you have upgraded every system to Windows 2000, you can make your life a little easier by removing WINS from your network.

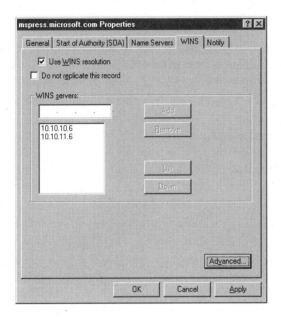

Figure 9-5.
It's simple to configure DNS to query a WINS database.

Before disabling the services, make sure you have removed all client dependencies. Verify that no client systems have a WINS server configured, or they will experience problems. Also, ensure that they have DNS servers specified—they will need some way of finding network resources. This is a simple process if you are using DHCP because you can simply reconfigure options at the DHCP server.

If you would like to completely disable NetBIOS on your network, you can do so. Start by removing WINS gradually. Instead of completely removing the services from each server, set the server to start up manually and stop the services. By leaving WINS on the server, you can start it again if you discover that you have not completely removed the WINS dependency. Once you have stopped all WINS services on your network, wait a few days to ensure that none of your users are experiencing problems because of the changes. After you are confident that the network is stable, you can actually remove WINS from your servers by using the Add/Remove Programs item in Control Panel.

Active Directory

The newest member of the Windows namespace is Active Directory. Active Directory allows clients to locate objects using Lightweight Directory Access Protocol (LDAP). The functionality provided by Active Directory will eventually replace WINS, allowing clients to easily locate any service within their network.

Beyond simply providing a namespace, Active Directory allows administrators great control over the organization of that namespace and what data is stored in it. Active Directory can be extended to meet a variety of requirements and can store a significant amount of data. Like WINS and DNS, Active Directory allows for both fail-over and redundancy by providing replication between multiple servers. Active Directory even allows updates to occur on any of the directory servers, an improvement over Windows NT 4.0 domain controllers.

Active Directory is such an important part of Windows networking that an entire chapter of this book has been dedicated to it. For more information on Active Directory, refer to Chapter 11.

DHCP (Dynamic Host Configuration Protocol)

One of the goals of Windows networking has been to make it easy for administrators to configure and manage their networks. DHCP, the Dynamic Host Configuration Protocol, simplifies the time-consuming task of setting IP addresses. DHCP allows an administrator to manage all IP addresses from a central server. When IP clients start up, they contact the server to determine their IP configuration. Windows 2000 Server can act as either a DHCP client or server.

DHCP makes networks easier to configure initially because Windows systems act as DHCP clients by default. Without DHCP, administrators would have to manually type in IP addresses for each system. While this is common practice, it is a very error-prone process.

Administrators will particularly appreciate DHCP the first time they need to reconfigure their network. An administrator can renumber a network segment and change DNS or WINS servers and many other client configurations from a central server. Without DHCP, each system on the network would need to be reconfigured individually and manually.

DHCP Concepts

There are several concepts that are specific to DHCP that you might not be familiar with. A *scope* is a group of IP addresses. Scope defines the range of IP addresses a DHCP server uses to assign clients' addresses as well as their configuration parameters. For example, a single scope could be defined as the IP addresses from 192.168.10.5 to 192.168.10.250, a DNS server with the IP address 192.168.10.4, a WINS server at 192.168.10.3, and a default gateway at 192.168.10.1.

Clients are assigned IP addresses for use over a specific period. This is called a *lease*. The metaphor continues—the client must renew a lease before it expires, normally halfway through the lease period. The lease period is configurable by the administrator. For example, the administrator could configure an eight-day lease period. After four days, the client would attempt to renew its lease so it could continue to use the same IP address.

Clients locate their DHCP server by sending a broadcast message to their local network. Broadcast messages do not cross routers, so it is important to have a system on each subnet listening for DHCP requests. *DHCP relay agents* can listen for these requests and forward them on to a DHCP server. DHCP relay agents allow each subnet to have a DHCP server without requiring a true DHCP server on each network.

Another option is to configure routers to forward DHCP requests. If the routers on your network support RFC 1542 or offer Bootstrap Protocol (BOOTP)–relay capabilities, enable this instead of using server-based DHCP relay agents.

New Features

DHCP continues to be an important part of the Zero Administration for Windows initiative. Many new features have been added to the DHCP services that were included with previous versions of Windows NT. These additions are described in the sections that follow.

Improved Management Utility

Naturally, DHCP management functions have been integrated into the MMC as a snap-in. The new snap-in provides some new features, as well. Icons used to identify scopes will change to indicate a warning or an error state when the scope begins to run out of free addresses. Figure 9-6 shows the new DHCP management utility.

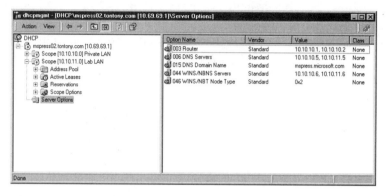

Figure 9-6.
The DHCP management utility is now an MMC snap-in.

DHCP and the Windows NT Namespace

DHCP allocates IP addresses for systems when they boot. This is important for directory services such as DNS and WINS because the database must be updated each time the system boots to remain accurate. WINS was designed to work with DHCP and integrates easily, but DNS is somewhat more complicated. DNS was designed long before DHCP became common on IP networks, and is intended to hold static data. Previous versions of Windows NT Server included interaction between WINS and DNS so that Microsoft-based DNS servers could look in the dynamic WINS database to find IP addresses. This was an excellent workaround, but did not suit those environments that relied on UNIX-based DNS.

The new DNS dynamic update protocol standards make it much easier for a DNS host name to follow a computer with a dynamically assigned IP address. The dynamic update database allows an update to occur at the moment the IP address is assigned to the client. This way, when a roving user moves from one subnet to another, his or her DNS host name remains the same.

New Default Behavior When No DHCP Server Is Found

Instead of starting without network capabilities, Windows 2000 DHCP clients will attempt to configure themselves if they cannot locate a DHCP server. The client will choose an IP address that does not conflict with any other system on the network. It will then attempt to contact a DHCP server every five minutes until it finds one. When it does find one, it will reconfigure itself according to the information provided by the server.

This is a great improvement over previous versions of Windows, which showed users an error message and stopped them from using anything on the network. A DHCP server failure will now have much less impact than it did previously. Now Windows 2000 clients will start up network services anyway and grab a valid configuration whenever possible—without ever alerting the user.

Active Directory Controlled Service

It is possible for a user running Windows 2000 Server on his or her desktop system to start the DHCP service. The user might do this to learn about DHCP, but the effects can be unpredictable. Client computers contact their DHCP server by sending out broadcast messages—those messages can be returned by any listening system, even one that was just set up for learning purposes. This can cause a problem because the configuration probably will not be correct.

When Windows 2000 Server is used with Active Directory, DHCP services contact Active Directory to determine whether they are authorized for that network. If the server that started the DHCP service is not on the list of authorized DHCP servers, Active Directory will stop the service automatically. This can avoid difficult-to-track problems caused by errant DHCP servers responding to client requests.

Audit Logging

DHCP has auditing capabilities that help administrators monitor the state of the DHCP server. These capabilities have been expanded to reduce the number of problems caused by the log files themselves. These new features ensure that logs will no longer fill partitions. There is no graphical user interface for these settings. To modify the values, edit the following registry key:

```
HKEY_LOCAL_MACHINE\SYSTEM\CurrentControlSet\Services\DHCPServer\Parameters
```

Table 9-1 shows some of the possible values for the Parameters registry key that control the DHCP auditing capabilities.

Values for the Parameters Registry Key

Value Name	Data Type	Description
DhcpLogFilePath	REG_SZ	Administrators can specify the partition and directory that audit logs will be written to. Set this value to the full path to which logs will be written.
DhcpLogMinSpaceOnDisk	REG_DWORD	Administrators can monitor free disk space. If the number of free megabytes on the disk falls below the number in this registry value, audit logging will stop.
DhcpLogDiskSpaceCheckInterval	REG_DWORD	The number of times the audit log will be written to before checking for free disk space.
DhcpLogFileMaxSize	REG_DWORD	Administrators can set a maximum size for all DHCP logs on the server, ensuring that the logs will not consume more than their fair share of space. This value is the number of megabytes, defaulting to 7.

Table 9-1.
Administrators must set registry values to control DHCP log settings.

Multicast DHCP

Multicast DHCP (MDHCP) is an entirely separate entity from DHCP that helps clients subscribe to multicast messages. Multicast messages use the Class D range of IP addresses from 224.0.0.0 to 239.255.255.255. Like the other aspects of Windows 2000 Server, multicast scopes are created using a wizard interface, as illustrated in Figure 9-7. Clients are required to have an ordinary IP address (assigned manually or by DHCP) before they can make use of multicast addressing. MDHCP is defined in RFCs 1541 and 2131.

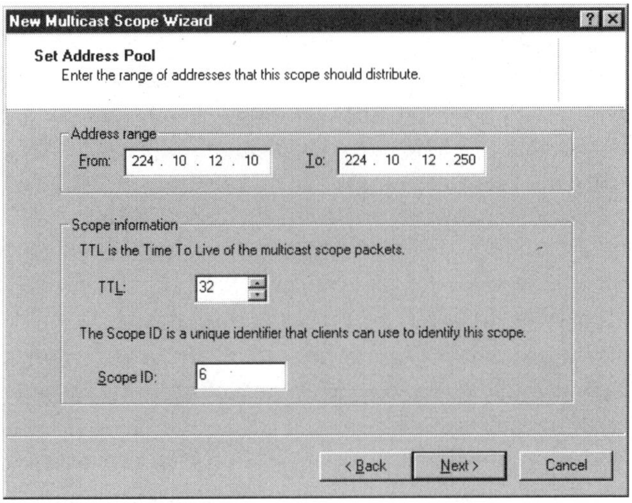

Figure 9-7.
Multicast scopes are created using a wizard interface.

Class Store

Built into Active Directory is a feature called the *Class Store*, which will redefine how applications are distributed. The Class Store is another type of namespace— it allows application components to be stored centrally on the network and retrieved only when needed by client systems. All data necessary for running an application can now be centralized in Active Directory.

This incredible technology changes many things about the way applications work in a network environment. Now a user can roam to any desktop system and have all his or her normal applications available—without manually installing them on other systems. The Windows 2000 system that the user logs into will contact the Active Directory server to find where it can get a copy of the necessary files, COM objects, and packages.

Besides helping roaming users, administrators will save time by upgrading a single copy of an application. By updating the application components stored in Active Directory, all clients can upgrade themselves the next time the application is launched. This will normally require no intervention from the end-user, either—finally allowing centralized software distribution with the performance benefit of storing the application on the local systems.

Summary

Microsoft has constantly improved its network services for the enterprise, as shown by the newest generation of distributed network services. By definition, distributed network services benefit large environments by providing redundancy, load-balancing, and localization of network traffic. Several of Windows 2000 Server's components meet these criteria, including WINS, DNS, Active Directory, and DHCP.

WINS has been relied upon for years to resolve NetBIOS names to IP addresses on Microsoft networks. The WINS included with Windows 2000 Server allows for backward compatibility with older Windows systems that still require NetBIOS communications. It even improves on previous generations of the service by making it more manageable.

DNS is the most important namespace on the Internet because it allows users to find servers using domain names such as www.microsoft.com. Windows 2000 Server provides DNS services that support extended features such as DNS dynamic update protocol and WINS integration.

Active Directory is the most extensive namespace ever and includes all objects on a Windows network.

DHCP is an essential part of reducing administration time for IP networks—it allows computers to be automatically configured and reconfigured. Windows 2000 adds several new features to DHCP, such as Multicast DHCP and an improved default behavior when no DHCP server is available.

The Microsoft Distributed File System (Dfs)

Overview

Many network administrators have experienced problems with the traditional concept of mapping a drive to a remote network share. First, since each drive being mapped requires a letter of the alphabet, the client is limited in the number of network connections it can establish. Second, users must track which servers contain which shares and create a separate connection for each server on which they want to use files.

The Distributed file system (Dfs) built into Microsoft Windows 2000 Server solves these problems and provides additional benefits through new features. Dfs allows an administrator to create a directory tree that can consist of shares from systems anywhere on the network. Users can access files anywhere on this directory tree, and their computers will automatically and transparently connect to the appropriate server. This allows clients to map a single network drive and connect to all the network resources the administrator has configured to be accessible through a given Dfs tree.

You should use Dfs in your network if file services extend beyond a few simple, unrelated shares.

Management of Dfs

Management of Dfs for Windows 2000 Server is done through the Distributed File System utility in the Administrative Tools program group, shown in Figure 10-1 on the following page. This tool provides a graphical interface to create replica sets, child nodes, and Dfs roots. It uses a wizard interface for most tasks, so it is simple to create and manage a Dfs tree. The Dfs roots you manage are stored as part of the MMC console file—remember to save the file after you have configured it to administer your Dfs roots!

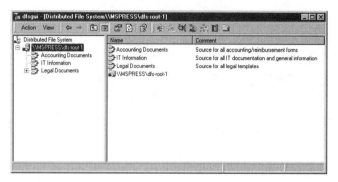

Figure 10-1.
The Dfs utility provides a GUI interface for managing Dfs trees.

Dfs Architecture and Features

With the traditional file-sharing mechanisms included in previous versions of Windows, the end user could connect to network file-sharing points in several ways. The most common mechanism was the Network Neighborhood, where a user could browse a list of servers and view the shares available on each of the servers. Users also had the option of connecting directly to a server and a share using the uniform naming convention (UNC). However, this option could be used only if users already knew where on the network they needed to connect. In both of these cases, the user's system took the same steps to initiate the connection—it established a session with the remote server and requested access to a specific share.

Dfs improves upon this architecture by building in more flexibility. In the simplest case, an administrator creates a Dfs root that acts exactly like a network share point. However, when the user chooses a subdirectory of the Dfs root, the client computer recognizes that it is not a true subdirectory but rather a placeholder for another network share. The client will then automatically connect to that network share—which might reside on an entirely different server—and display the files within it to the user.

This architecture allows a single Dfs root to give a user access to all the file servers in an enterprise. Dfs services with this level of functionality were available as an add-on to Windows NT 4.0. Another free add-on allowed Windows 95 clients to connect to these Dfs roots. Windows 98 and Windows NT 4.0 have the client functionality built in.

Windows 2000 Server extends the scope of Dfs. Using Active Directory, Dfs root information no longer needs to reside on a single server. Windows 2000 clients can connect to Active Directory and retrieve a list of potential Dfs root servers. The clients can use the information in Active Directory to automatically connect to the closest system geographically, thereby reducing the burden on the network. The clients will automatically connect to another Dfs root server if the closest server is not available. The ability to host multiple Dfs root servers provides for both load balancing and redundancy.

Load balancing and redundancy can also be used for nested shares within the Dfs root. A user who accesses a subdirectory of the Dfs tree can be redirected to one of several servers. In this way, different parts of the Dfs tree can have various levels of fail-over capabilities. To complement these features, Dfs includes a replication component to ensure that data between multiple servers is synchronized according to the administrator's specifications. Clients can use the site information contained in Active Directory to locate the nearest server hosting a given share.

Improved and Simplified Access to Data

The Dfs tree is not limited to Windows 2000 Servers. Any Microsoft system capable of sharing files (such as Windows for Workgroups, Windows 95, Windows 98, and Windows NT systems) can be included as a leaf node in a Dfs tree. Even NetWare, Banyan, Macintosh, and UNIX systems can be included as leaf nodes on a Dfs tree if they have the proper software! Resources on each of these types of systems will be accessible transparently by the end user. Figure 10-2 on the following page shows a client's view of a Dfs tree sharing resources from multiple servers using multiple operating systems.

Not all systems can participate as Dfs clients, however. Dfs relies on the client to choose among multiple servers, so accessing a Dfs root requires special client software. Fortunately, Windows 98, Windows NT 4.0 Workstation, and Windows NT 4.0 Server include Dfs client software. Microsoft makes available a free client for Windows 95 that can be downloaded and installed. Even with the special client, Windows 95 systems have a unique restriction—a Windows 95 client can traverse a Dfs tree, but it cannot enter a section of the tree that the client itself shares out. If you have ever tried to connect to a share located on your own Windows 95 system, you already know that it does not allow self-referential share connection.

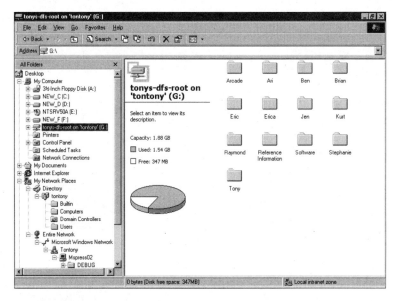

Figure 10-2.
From Windows Explorer, Dfs trees look like any other share.

Fault Tolerance and Load Balancing

Besides just making it easier for clients to get to data on the network, Dfs helps networks scale upward by providing for fault tolerance and load balancing. To provide this, administrators can configure multiple Windows 2000 Servers to share the same Dfs root. When a client connects to a Dfs tree shared by multiple servers, Active Directory notifies the client software about each of the servers that share that same tree. The client has the option of connecting to any one of the servers. If one of the servers does not respond, the client will automatically fail-over to a different server.

Because clients can connect to multiple Windows 2000 servers sharing the same data, even if your entire network were part of a single Dfs tree no single server would be burdened with supporting the entire network—Dfs distributes the load placed on a Dfs network share among multiple servers. Further, clients use Active Directory site information to connect to the closest server, reducing the load on the network infrastructure. Thus, Dfs reduces the load both on any given server and on the underlying network. While clients accessing the file server will generate less traffic, there is additional overhead caused by replicating content. Exactly how much overhead the updates add depends entirely on the frequency.

Dfs trees operate in one of two modes: fault tolerant or stand-alone. When configured for fault tolerance, the topology of the tree is actually stored within Active Directory. Hence, the Dfs tree benefits from the inherent redundancy built into your network's Active Directory. Stand-alone Dfs trees are launched from a single server and become unavailable if that server fails.

When a client connects to a fault-tolerant Dfs node using the DNS domain name, Active Directory forwards to the client a list of servers that have a replica of the content. If the first server the client attempts to connect to is unavailable, the client has the intelligence to try each server in the list until it succeeds in connecting to one.

Fail-over between replicated network shares is entirely transparent because Dfs hides the underlying process from the user. Users do not lose the ability to connect directly to a specific server's Dfs root—they simply connect using the UNC path as they would in mapping a drive to a regular share.

Replication

The Dfs add-on that Microsoft distributed for use with Windows NT 4.0 included the fault-tolerance and load-balancing features described in the previous section. However, it lacked an essential part of making those features useful—replication. Some mechanism must keep the data synchronized in order for multiple servers to provide the same share.

Fortunately, Windows 2000 Server allows replication to occur between Dfs roots and between child nodes. Replicas are created using the Dfs snap-in. Figure 10-3 on the following page shows a Dfs root replicated between three servers. Be sure to use NTFS dynamic volumes to host all replicas—replicas will not work with FAT partitions or even with Windows NT 4.0–compatible NTFS partitions.

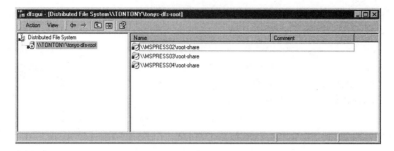

Figure 10-3.
Multiple servers can host replicated copies of a Dfs root.

The File Replication Service handles the synchronization of data between shares that participate in the same replica. The File Replication Service automatically replicates files when they are modified and closed. By default, it synchronizes replica schedules every 15 minutes. Please note that replication does not occur constantly—there is no guarantee that data will be completely consistent between the members of a replica set. You must be willing to tolerate some lag time while changes propagate.

The cache settings control exactly how long the lag time will be. Set the cache timeout according to how often users update files. Replica sets containing frequently changing data require a short cache timeout. A longer cache timeout is acceptable when documents are rarely updated.

Integration with the Windows NT Security Model

Participating in a Dfs tree does not override share-level security. Each system that participates in a Dfs tree controls which users have access to the resources on the system. This allows departments that have different system administrators to participate in a single tree—each administrator retains full control over the content published by his or her file servers.

Summary

Distributed file system will change the way Windows systems network. Now users can access an entire network of resources without having any knowledge of the underlying system or network architecture. Availability is increased, too, if administrators choose to use Active Directory to enable replication between multiple servers. Backward compatibility with Windows NT 4.0, Windows 95, and Windows 98 ensures that networks can immediately benefit from Dfs.

CHAPTER ELEVEN

Active Directory

Overview

Keeping track of everything on your network is a time-consuming task. Even on small networks, users tend to have difficulty finding network file and printer shares. Without some kind of network directory, medium and large networks are *impossible* to manage, and users will often have a difficult time finding resources on the network.

Previous versions of Microsoft Windows included services to help users and administrators find network resources. Network Neighborhood is useful in many environments, but users often complain about the clumsy interface, and its unpredictability baffles many administrators. The WINS Manager and Server Manager could be used to view a list of systems on the network, but they were not readily available to end users. Administrators utilized User Manager to add and delete users, an entirely different type of network object. These applications got the job done, but proved to be inefficient—especially in large networks.

All of these objects resided in a common container: the Microsoft Windows NT domain. Windows NT domains worked best in small-sized and medium-sized environments. Administrators of large environments were forced to partition their network into multiple domains interconnected with trusts. Microsoft Windows 2000 Server introduces Active Directory to replace domain functionality. Active Directory will continue to get the job done, but in a much more efficient way. Active Directory can be replicated between multiple domain controllers, so no single system is critical. In this way, the crucial data stored within Active Directory is both redundant and load-balanced.

A directory, in the most generic sense, is a comprehensive listing of objects. A phone book is a type of directory that stores information about people, businesses, and government organizations. Phone books typically record names, addresses, and phone numbers. Active Directory is similar to a phone book in several ways, and it is far more flexible. Active Directory will store information about organizations, sites, systems, users, shares, and just about any other network object that you can imagine. Not all objects are as similar to each other as those stored in the phone book, so Active Directory includes the ability to record different types of information about different objects. This chapter will teach you

- What Active Directory is
- How standard protocols like DNS dynamic update protocol and Lightweight Directory Access Protocol (LDAP) are used
- How to plan for migrating to Active Directory
- What objects, schema, object classes, and attributes are
- How replication and partitioning work
- What the global catalog is useful for and how to use it

Active Directory Components

As I mentioned in the introduction, Active Directory stores information about network components. It allows clients to find objects within its *namespace*. The term namespace (also known as *console tree*) refers to the area in which a network component can be located. For example, the table of contents of this book forms a namespace in which chapters can be resolved to page numbers. DNS is a namespace that resolves host names to IP addresses. Telephone books provide a namespace for resolving names to telephone numbers. Active Directory provides a namespace for resolving the names of network objects to the objects themselves. Active Directory can resolve a wide range of objects, including users, systems, and services on a network.

Everything that Active Directory tracks is considered an *object*. An object is any user, system, resource, or service tracked within Active Directory. The generic term *object* is used because Active Directory is capable of tracking a variety of items, and many objects can share common *attributes*.

Attributes describe objects in Active Directory. For example, all User objects share attributes to store a user name, full name, and description. Systems are also objects, but they have a separate set of attributes that include a host name, an IP address, and a location.

The set of attributes available for any particular object type is called a *schema*. The schema makes object classes different from each other. Schema information is actually stored within Active Directory, which allows administrators to add attributes to object classes and have them distributed across the network to all corners of the domain, without restarting any domain controllers.

A *container* is a special type of object used to organize Active Directory. It does not represent anything physical, like a user or a system. Instead, it is used to group other objects. Container objects can be nested within other containers.

Each object in an Active Directory has a *name*. These are not the names that you are accustomed to, like "Tony" or "Eric." They are LDAP *distinguished names*. LDAP distinguished names are complicated, but they allow any object within a directory to be identified uniquely regardless of its type. My distinguished name on the Microsoft network is "/O=Internet/DC=COM/DC=Microsoft/DC=MSPress/CN=Users/CN=Tony Northrup"...but you can call me Tony.

The term *tree* is used to describe a set of objects within Active Directory. When containers and objects are combined hierarchically, they tend to form branches—hence the term. A related term is *contiguous subtree*, which refers to an unbroken branch of the tree.

Continuing the tree metaphor, the term *forest* describes trees that are not part of the same namespace but that share a common schema, configuration, and global catalog. Trees in a forest all trust each other, so objects in these trees are available to all users if the security allows it. Organizations that are divided into multiple domains should group the trees into a single forest.

A *site* is a geographical location, as defined within Active Directory. Sites correspond to logical IP subnets, and as such, they can be used by applications to locate the closest server on a network. Using site information from Active Directory can profoundly reduce the traffic on wide area networks.

Managing Active Directory

The Active Directory Users and Computers MMC snap-in is the most useful tool for administering your Active Directory. It is directly accessible from the Administrative Tools program group on the Start menu. It replaces and improves upon Server Manager and User Manager from Windows NT 4.0. Take a few minutes to familiarize yourself with this tool. It is very intuitive—just be sure not to make any modifications until you understand how Active Directory works.

Security

Active Directory plays an important role in the future of Windows networking. Administrators must be able to protect their directory from attackers and users, while delegating tasks to other administrators where necessary. This is all possible using the Active Directory security model, which associates an access control list (ACL) with each container, object, and object attribute within the directory. Figure 11-1 shows a step from the Delegation Of Control wizard, a helpful utility for assigning permissions to Active Directory objects.

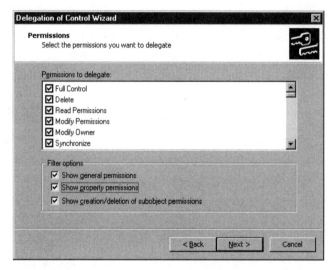

Figure 11-1.
The Delegation Of Control wizard makes it simple to assign permissions to objects.

This high level of control allows an administrator to grant individual users and groups varying levels of permissions for objects and their properties. Administrators can even add attributes to objects and hide those attributes from certain groups of users. For example, the administrator could set the ACLs such that only managers can view the home phone numbers of other users. Nonmanagers would not even know that the attribute existed.

A concept new to Windows 2000 Server is *delegated administration*. This allows administrators to assign administrative tasks to other users, while not granting those users more power than necessary. Delegated administration can be assigned over specific objects or contiguous subtrees of a directory. This is a much more effective method of giving authority over the networks; rather than granting someone the all powerful Domain Administrator permissions, he or she can be given permissions for just those systems and users within a specific subtree. Active Directory supports *inheritance*, so any new objects inherit the ACL of their container.

Try to forget what you've learned about Windows NT domain trusts. The term *trusts* is still used, but trusts have very different functionality. There is no distinction between one-way and two-way trusts because all Active Directory trusts are bidirectional. Further, all trusts are transitive. So, if Domain A trusts Domain B, and Domain B trusts Domain C, then there is an automatic implicit trust between Domain A and Domain C. This new functionality is shown in Figure 11-2.

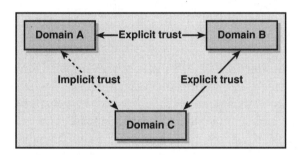

Figure 11-2.
Windows 2000 Server trusts are bidirectional and transitive.

Another Active Directory security feature is auditing. Just as you can audit NTFS partitions, objects and containers within Active Directory can be audited. This is a useful way to determine who is attempting to access objects, and whether or not they succeed.

Use of DNS (Domain Name System)

Domain Name System, or DNS, is necessary to any Internet-connected organization. DNS provides name resolution between common names, such as mspress.microsoft.com, and the raw IP addresses that network layer components use to communicate. Active Directory makes extensive use of DNS technology and relies on DNS to locate objects within Active Directory. This is a substantial change from previous Windows operating systems that require NetBIOS names to be resolved to IP addresses, and to rely on WINS or another NetBIOS name resolution technique.

Active Directory works best when used with Windows 2000–based DNS servers. Microsoft has made it easy for administrators to transition to Windows 2000–based DNS servers by providing migration wizards that walk the administrator through the process. Other DNS servers can be used, but administrators will need to spend more time managing the DNS databases. If you decide not to use Windows 2000–based DNS servers, you should make sure your DNS servers comply with the new DNS dynamic update protocol. Active Directory servers rely on dynamic update to update their pointer records, and clients rely on these records to locate domain controllers. If dynamic update is not supported, you will have to update the databases manually.

NOTE: DNS dynamic update protocol is defined in RFC 2136.

Windows domains and Internet domains are now completely compatible. A domain name such as mspress.microsoft.com will identify Active Directory domain controllers responsible for the domain, so any client with DNS access can locate a domain controller. Active Directory clients can use DNS resolution to locate any number of services because Active Directory servers publish a list of addresses to DNS using the new features of dynamic update. These addresses identify both the domain and the service being provided and are published via Service Resource Records (SRV RRs). SRV RRs follow this format:

```
service.protocol.domain
```

Active Directory servers provide the LDAP service for object location, and LDAP relies on TCP as the underlying transport-layer protocol. Therefore, a client searching for an Active Directory server within the mspress.microsoft.com domain would look up the DNS record for ldap.tcp.mspress.microsoft.com.

Global Catalog

Active Directory provides a *global catalog* (GC). No, this does not mean that you can find any piece of information on the planet—but it is still very significant. Active Directory provides a single source to locate any object within an organization's network.

The global catalog is a service within Windows 2000 Server that allows users to find any objects to which they have been granted access. This functionality far surpasses that of the Find Computer application included in previous versions of Windows, because users can search for any object within Active Directory: servers, printers, users, and applications. For example, Figure 11-3 shows how a user can search for all color printers in his or her building that have the capability to print double-sided documents.

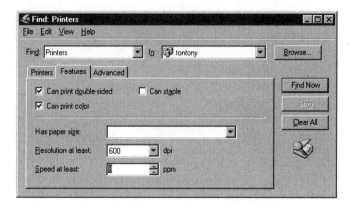

Figure 11-3.
The global catalog helps users find network resources.

This feature is especially important because of the complexity of LDAP names. Older versions of Windows relied on 15-character NetBIOS computer names, which users could often remember. Few people would be able to recall LDAP names, such as the following:

```
/O=Internet/DC=COM/DC=Microsoft/DC=MSPress/CN=Computers/CN=Server1.
```

Because users can easily search for objects, remembering names is much less important.

The GC is an index stored on Active Directory servers. It contains the names of all objects in the Active Directory server, regardless of how the server has been partitioned. The GC also contains a handful of searchable attributes for each object. For example, the GC would store the distinguished names, first names, and last names of all users—allowing someone to search for anyone named Tony and find the distinguished name of the user. The global catalog is a subset of Active Directory, and stores only those attributes that users tend to search on. Useful defaults are provided by Microsoft, and administrators can specify other attributes to be searchable by using the Active Directory Schema, described later in this chapter.

Not All Indexes Are Created Equal!

If you have done any database administration, you already know that some types of information are more useful to index than other types. Naturally, you should index attributes that will be searched for often, but there are other factors involved. Indexes take up space, so it is not efficient to index everything. Indexes also slow down updates and inserts—if an indexed attribute is modified, the index must be modified as well. Indexing works better when the data being stored varies from user to user. Therefore, never index true or false attributes or any attribute with less than five possible values. Names are an excellent attribute to index since they are almost unique for each user. Finally, don't index attributes that aren't usually filled in. If few users enter a value for their middle name, the indexing of that attribute is a waste.

As new objects are created in Active Directory, they are assigned a unique number called a GUID (globally unique identifier). The GUID is useful because it stays the same for any given object, regardless of where the object is moved. The GUID is a 128-bit identifier, which isn't particularly meaningful to users, but applications that reference objects in Active Directory can record the GUIDs for objects and use the global catalog to find them even after they've moved.

Replication

Administrators who implement Active Directory will quickly discover that their network relies heavily on its services. This reliance means that Active Directory must be available on multiple servers—so that if a single server fails, clients can contact a server with duplicate services and information. Unlike the Windows NT domain databases used with previous versions of Windows NT, updates to the database can be sent to *any* of the Active Directory servers. While this complicates the replication process, it eliminates the possibility that the failure of a single domain controller would stop updates to the databases. It also reduces the high load placed on Windows NT 4.0 primary domain controllers.

Windows 2000 Server includes a replication component within the suite of Active Directory services that makes this a simple task for administrators. Simply adding domain controllers to an Active Directory domain is sufficient to begin the replication process.

One of the most complex parts of making redundant servers work properly is replicating the information and ensuring that all servers have the most up-to-date content. Active Directory uses *multimaster replication,* which is another way of stating that updates can occur on any Active Directory server. Each server keeps track of which updates it has received from which servers, and can intelligently request only necessary updates in case of a failure.

How Active Directory Replication Works

Active Directory replication will seem logical if you're already familiar with how replication works in Windows NT 4.0 domains. Each update is assigned its own 64-bit unique sequence number (USN) from a counter that is incremented whenever a change is made. These updates are system-specific, so every Active Directory server maintains a separate counter.

When a server replicates an update to other Active Directory servers, it sends the USN along with the change. Each server maintains an internal list of replication partners and the highest USN received from them. The server receiving the update requests only those changes with USNs higher than previously received. This method has the added benefit of stopping updates from propagating endlessly between multiple Active Directory servers.

One problem inherent in any multimaster replication scheme is that updates to a single object can occur in multiple places at the same time. For example, if an administrator in Boston changes a user's name from "Curt" to "'Kurt" and an administrator in Chicago simultaneously changes that same user's name from "Curt" to "Kirk," a replication collision will occur. There are two problems to deal with when a collision occurs: detecting the collision and resolving the collision.

Active Directory stores *property version numbers* to allow replication collision detection. These numbers are specific to each property of every object within Active Directory and are updated every time the property is modified. These numbers are propagated through Active Directory along with the change, so a server that receives two different updates to the same property with the same property version number can conclude that a replication collision has occurred.

Active Directory servers resolve collisions by applying the update with the later timestamp. The timestamp is created by the server that initiated the change, so it is very important to keep system time synchronized between Windows 2000 servers.

NOTE: Use the built-in distributed time synchronization service to keep all servers working together!

Partitioning

Large networks can contain hundreds of thousands of objects. Windows NT required multiple domains to allow that many objects to be manageable. Administrators often divided users and resources into separate domains and created a trust between the domains. The structure of the databases simply did not allow them to grow to hundreds of thousands of objects. These size limitations are less a factor in Active Directory domains, thankfully. However, supporting a very large Active Directory could be an incredible burden to any single domain controller.

Active Directories can be partitioned to lessen this load. Partitioning allows different domain controllers to manage different sections of the database, reducing the load on any individual server. The clients can use resources located within different Active Directory partitions transparently. Therefore, administrators can manage massive Active Directory domains without requiring domain controllers to handle the entire database.

Schema: Attributes and Object Classes

As I defined the term earlier, a schema is a set of attributes used to describe a particular object class in Active Directory. Different types of information need to be tracked for different object classes, and that's why the schema is so important. For example, the Users object class needs attributes for a first name, last name, phone number, e-mail address, and mailing address. The Printer object class must have many different attributes—users will want to know how fast a printer is and whether it can duplex or print in color. These attributes can be viewed and edited using the Active Directory Schema MMC snap-in, as shown in Figure 11-4. The Active Directory Schema does not have an icon within the Start menu; you must launch the MMC interface and add the snap-in named Active Directory Schema.

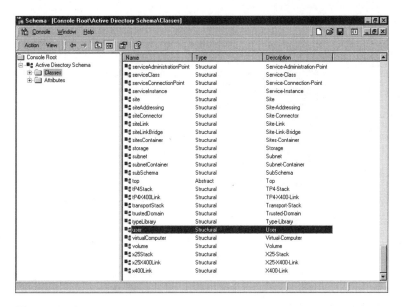

Figure 11-4.
The Active Directory Schema allows classes and attributes to be modified.

By default, object classes come with a logical set of attributes that will fit most organization's needs. However, many organizations will need to track additional information about particular object classes. For example, if employees are assigned a badge number, it is useful to track that information in the object class. The first step is to create an attribute called BadgeID, as shown in Figure 11-5 on the next page. The second step is to make the new attribute optional for the Users class.

Figure 11-5.
Attributes can be added with the Active Directory Schema snap-in.

The schema is stored within Active Directory just like other objects. Therefore, the schema inherits the ability to be automatically replicated throughout a domain. It also benefits from the security features of Active Directory, and allows administrators to delegate authority over the schema to different users and groups. By changing the ACLs on a schema object, an administrator can allow any user to add or modify attributes for an object class. The example in Figure 11-6 shows that the group East Coast Administrators has been granted full control over the schema.

Editing the Schema Isn't All *That* Easy!

By default, Active Directory servers do not allow the schema to be edited. Before this can be done, you must add a REG_DWORD value to the Registry named Schema Update Allowed and set it to 1. This value should be added to the following Registry key:

```
\HKLM\SYSTEM\CurrentControlSet\Services\NTDS\Parameters
```

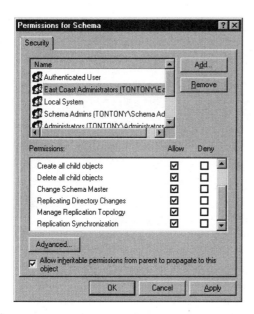

Figure 11-6.
Modifying the schema can be delegated to groups and users.

New attributes have several properties that must be set. The user creating a new attribute must define a name for the attribute (such as Badge ID #), the type of data to be stored (such as a string or a number), and the range limits (such as string length). A unique Object Identifier (OID) must also be provided. New attributes can be indexed, which adds the attributes to the global catalog. Indexes should be created for attributes that users will search with. In this example, if security needs to look up user accounts by the Badge ID number, this attribute should be indexed. For a search to occur on a nonindexed attribute, a slow and processor-intensive walk of the directory tree must be done.

You cannot delete a class or an attribute with the Active Directory Schema or any other tool. Once you create them, they will exist forever within your Active Directory. The only option you have is to deactivate a class, which stops it from being used in the future. You cannot deactivate a class or an attribute that has dependencies within Active Directory. For example, if an attribute is still used by an active class, that attribute must remain active.

Where Do Object Identifiers Come From?

The only way to ensure Object Identifiers are globally unique is to have a central agency that assigns OIDs. This is already common practice on the Internet; the InterNIC assigns domain names and the Internet Assigned Numbers Authority (IANA) assigns IP subnets. Object Identifiers are assigned by a National Registration Authority, or NRA. NRAs vary from country to country. In the United States, the American National Standards Institute (ANSI) provides NRA services. For a modest fee, ANSI can supply your organization with a root OID. Any objects created by your organization will have this root OID as the prefix, ensuring that Object Identifiers are globally unique.

A list of NRAs can be found at the International Standards Organization's Web site, at *http://www.iso.ch*.

The schema is cached by Active Directory servers for performance reasons. It will take up to five minutes for the cache to be updated after you change the schema. So, wait a few minutes before you try to create objects based on your new object classes and attributes. If you must reload the cache immediately, add the attribute schemaUpdateNow to the root object (the object without a distinguished name), and set the value to 1.

Extending the schema of Active Directory is a powerful capability. However, most administrators will never need to use anything but the classes and attributes Microsoft has provided by default.

Objects

Many people are initially confused by the relationship between object classes, attributes, and the objects themselves. Objects are created based on an object class. Attributes describe an object class. When an object is created, it inherits all the attributes of its object class. Here's where it gets tricky: *object classes and attributes are also objects in Active Directory*. Fortunately, most user interfaces hide this fact.

An object can be either a reference to something concrete or the actual useful information itself. For example, every bit of information about a user account is stored within Active Directory. However, only a reference to a disk volume is stored in Active Directory. While the reference is not useful by itself, it is used to locate the volume on the file server. When creating new object classes, carefully consider whether the object will store a reference to something external or whether all necessary information will be contained in the object's attributes. While Active Directory is extremely convenient, it should not be used to store large amounts of information, constantly changing information, or rarely used information.

Anytime you add a user or a computer to Active Directory, you are creating an object. Creating an object is often referred to as *publishing,* because it kicks off a process of replicating the new information across all Active Directory servers in the domain.

Standard Object Classes

Windows 2000 Server relies on Active Directory to store a great deal of useful information about users, groups, and machine accounts, which are of particular interest to administrators because they will be the most commonly accessed parts of Active Directory. The new user interface might not seem intuitive if you're an administrator of previous versions of Windows NT, but once you spend some time with it, things will be easier.

Users

User accounts are no longer managed using a dedicated utility. Instead, administrators use the Active Directory Users and Computers MMC snap-in, as shown in Figure 11-7 on the next page. The user accounts themselves have changed significantly, as well. Windows NT 4.0 simply tracks the user name, full name, description, password, and a handful of other attributes for each user. Windows 2000 Server takes advantage of Active Directory to extend these attributes. You can now use Active Directory to track a great deal of personal information about people, including phone number, address, and manager name. All of this additional information is entirely optional.

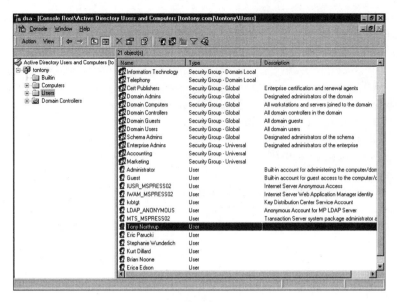

Figure 11-7.
The Active Directory Users and Computers snap-in replaces the User Manager.

Groups

Active Directory groups are similar to user groups in previous versions of Windows NT. However, they have a couple of new features as well. The newest version of Microsoft Exchange allows groups to be used as e-mail distribution lists. To make this more useful, e-mail accounts can be added to the groups to allow distribution to users who are not members of the same Active Directory tree. Groups can also be nested within each other. This will greatly reduce the amount of time administrators spend managing users and groups.

There are now three distinct types of user groups. Universal Groups will be the most commonly used type, and can contain users and other groups from anywhere in the forest. They are replicated outside of the domain and appear in the global catalog. Global Groups can only contain users and groups from the same domain. Global Groups are listed in the global catalog, but their membership list does not leave the domain. Domain Local Groups can only be applied to ACLs (access control lists) within the same domain but can contain users and groups from other domains. They are neither replicated outside of the domain nor listed in the global catalog. Any of these types of groups can participate in domain security or merely function as a distribution list.

Many groups are provided by Windows 2000 Server by default. These groups are called the *built-in* groups, and are pictured in Figure 11-8. Administrators can use these default groups for most purposes, and can add their own groups as needed.

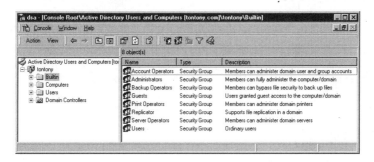

Figure 11-8.
Windows 2000 Server provides many built-in groups.

Machine Accounts

Systems that join a domain are automatically given a computer account in Active Directory. This is similar to adding a system to a Windows NT 4.0 domain. However, systems can be added to the domain even if they do not participate in domain security. For example, a computer object can be created for a UNIX system to help the administrators track that system.

Lightweight Directory Access Protocol (LDAP)

Active Directory reflects Microsoft's trend toward relying on standard protocols. The Lightweight Directory Access Protocol (LDAP) is a product of the IETF (Internet Engineering Task Force). It defines how clients and servers exchange information about a directory. LDAP version 2 and version 3 are used by Windows 2000 Server's Active Directory.

Distinguished Names

It is very important to understand the structure of distinguished names, as you will be referring to them often in the course of your job. My distinguished name is /O=Internet/DC=COM/DC=Microsoft/DC=MSPress/CN=Users/ CN=Tony Northrup. Consider Figure 11-9, which shows how I fit into a sample Active Directory tree. The distinguished name I gave starts to make some sense—it identifies each container from the very top down to my specific object. Each container is separated by a slash and an identifier. For example, COM, Microsoft, and MSPress are each preceded by /DC=. The DC stands for Domain Component, which identifies a DNS domain.

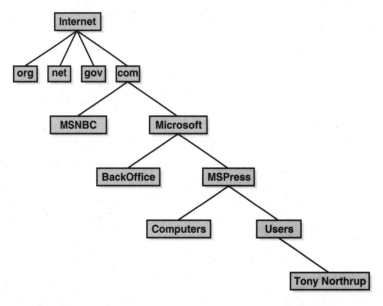

Figure 11-9.
Distinguished names describe the location of an object in a tree.

To simplify distinguished names, relative distinguished names can also be used. The relative distinguished name of the previous example is CN=Tony Northrup, identifying the user name but not the context in which it resides. The context must be known already for the relative distinguished name to be an effective identifier.

User Principal Name

Distinguished names are great for computers but too cumbersome for people to remember. People have grown accustomed to e-mail addresses, so Active Directory provides these addresses as a shortcut to the full object name. In Figure 11-9, Tony Northrup is a user of the mspress.microsoft.com domain. An administrator could create a user principal name within the microsoft.com domain to allow simpler access to my user account and hold a place for my e-mail address, like northrup@microsoft.com.

Users will rely on their user principal name to log onto their Windows 2000 systems. In other words, user principal names will replace the user names used in older Windows networks. Obviously, this helps the users by saving them the trouble of typing their distinguished names. However, it also benefits users because the user principal name will stay the same even if administrators move or rename the underlying user account.

ADSI (Active Directory Service Interface)

ADSI (Active Directory Service Interface) allows applications to interact with any directory service without being forced to know the internal details of the underlying protocols. Administrators can write programs and scripts that make use of ADSI to read or write to legacy Windows NT 4.0 directories, NetWare NDS directories, NetWare 3 binderies, and LDAP directories such as Active Directory. Developers can even create applications that make use of directories at the customer's site, without previous knowledge of the type of directory being used.

For example, the following Microsoft Visual Basic code uses ADSI to display a list of users in the debug window:

```
Set ou = GetObject("LDAP://dcserver/OU=Sales,DC=ArcadiaBay,DC=COM")
For Each obj In ou
    Debug.Print obj.Name
Next
```

As you can see, gathering a list of users is much simpler than in previous Windows operating systems. ADSI makes use of the Component Object Model (COM), so almost any Windows development environment can immediately make use of the interface. Developers will be interested to know that they can access Active Directory through the LDAP C API and through MAPI, though ADSI is the preferred interface.

NOTE: The LDAP C API is defined in RFC 1823.

Planning Your Network for Active Directory

Clients rely on site information to identify the closest Active Directory server. Because sites correspond to IP subnets, you should place Active Directory servers on each subnet. You should also make sure that all systems on the same logical subnet are connected via LAN hardware. Some routing technologies, such as Proxy Address Resolution Protocol (ARP), can allow systems to be on the same logical subnet but different physical network segments. This setup will trick clients into thinking systems are closer than they really are, so it's best to stick to standard routing techniques. If this isn't making much sense, that's okay—your network is probably set up just fine.

Make sure you have planned your Active Directory structure before you start migrating your network. You'll be given the option of creating a new tree or joining an existing tree. Obviously, if you're the first domain in the network to be migrated, you'll want to create a new tree. However, if you are merging multiple domains into a single Active Directory domain, you will want to join as a child of the existing tree.

Always migrate the Windows NT 3.51 or 4.0 PDC (Primary Domain Controller) to Windows 2000 Server Active Directory first. Users and groups from your current domain will be automatically transferred into Active Directory, and existing clients will interface with the new domain controller exactly as if it were still a PDC. As long as you have both Active Directory servers and legacy BDCs (backup domain controllers) in operation simultaneously, your domain will function as a *mixed mode domain*, as illustrated in Figure 11-10. Mixed domains cannot take full advantage of the new Active Directory features because Active Directory must ensure backward compatibility. For example, you cannot use nested groups in mixed mode domains.

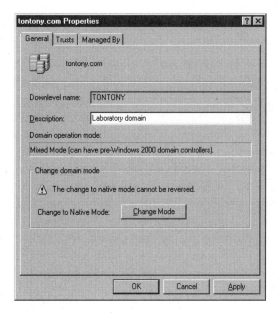

Figure 11-10.
Mixed mode domains are used when legacy BDCs still exist.

You should migrate the BDCs once you are sure the mixed mode domain is functioning completely. When all domain controllers have been migrated, you can switch the domain to *native mode,* reboot the domain controllers, and take full advantage of the new features. Member servers and workstations are completely supported and require no changes to interact with Active Directory servers. You will realize more benefits by upgrading the member servers as well, but always start by upgrading domain controllers.

Windows NT Workstation clients should be upgraded to Windows 2000 Professional to take advantage of the new features of Active Directory. A service pack will be made available for Microsoft Windows 95 and Windows 98 clients that will make them Active Directory–aware and allow them to participate in Kerberos security.

Summary

The addition of Active Directory to Windows 2000 Server is the most significant reason to upgrade your network. Active Directory combines Windows NT domains with Internet domains and makes them scalable to enterprise proportions. While the most significant benefit will be the reduced cost of ownership, users will directly benefit from the advanced search capabilities of the global catalog.

Active Directory is both standards-based and flexible. It's based on the LDAP standard, which has already been adopted by Cisco for use on network hardware and UNIX systems. The flexibility will be appreciated by any administrator who needs more functionality than is provided out of the box.

Microsoft wants it to be as easy as possible to migrate to Active Directory. Wizards are provided to transfer DNS responsibilities to Microsoft DNS dynamic update protocol servers. Users and groups from legacy Windows NT domains are automatically imported. Finally, every aspect of Active Directory setup is intuitive and GUI-oriented, and handles most complexities automatically.

Preparing for Windows 2000 Server

Overview

Now that you have mastered the features and technologies included with Microsoft Windows 2000 Server, you can begin implementing it in your network. Careful planning now can save a great deal of time and energy in the future, and this chapter will guide you through the process.

This chapter also provides detailed instructions on using the setup routine and points you toward other resources you might need to efficiently deploy Windows 2000 in your network.

Single Machine Installation

The simplest way to install Windows 2000 on a single system is to put the CD-ROM directly into the system's CD drive. If a Windows operating system is already installed on the computer, inserting the CD should bring up a prompt to upgrade the system. If you decide to start the setup process manually, execute winnt32.exe if you are using Windows 95, Windows 98, or Windows NT 4.0. From any other operating system, run winnt.exe.

If this is the first operating system to be installed on the computer, you must boot from either the CD-ROM or the floppy disks. Many new computers allow booting directly from the CD-ROM, which provides a very quick upgrade path. Alternatively, you can insert the first of the four setup floppy disks and follow the instructions to install the operating system.

winnt Command Syntax

Run winnt.exe from the command prompt to start the Windows 2000 setup routine from an MS-DOS, Windows 3.1, or Windows for Workgroups 3.11 system. The winnt.exe program accepts many different command-line parameters that change the behavior of setup and optionally automate the process. The following parameters can be used:

- /u:answer_file specifies an unattended install using an answer file. Answer files are used to bypass the interactive questions asked of the user and can even be used to automate the setup process completely.

- /e specifies a command to be executed after setup has completed. This can be used to launch automated application setup routines to complete the installation.

- /s:sourcepath specifies the path to the Windows 2000 setup files. This option is required only if the files are not located in the current folder.

- /t:tempdrive specifies which partition setup will use to store temporary files. This option is not recommended.

- /rx:folder copies a folder you create into the system folder. This option is generally used to copy drivers that are not part of the standard Windows 2000 distribution. This option can be used multiple times to copy multiple folders.

- /r:folder specifies that a folder be created during setup. This option can be used multiple times to create multiple folders.

- /a allows you to choose accessibility options. This option is not recommended for most users.

- /i:inffile specifies the file name of the setup information file. By default, this is Dosnet.inf. This option is not recommended.

NOTE: The command line options listed for winnt.exe are the ones that were available at the time this book was written.

winnt32 Command Syntax

Run winnt32.exe to start the Windows 2000 setup routine from a Windows 95, Windows 98, Windows NT 3.51, or Windows NT 4.0 command prompt. The winnt32.exe program can accept many different command-line parameters that change the behavior of setup and, optionally, automate the process. The following parameters can be used:

- /debug[level][:filename] creates a debug log file containing information at a specific level. If you do not specify a level, 2 will be used. Level 2 records warning information. If you do not specify a filename, the log file will be written to C:\winnt32.log. Use of this option is recommended because the log file can be used to diagnose setup problems.

- /s:sourcepath specifies the path to the Windows 2000 setup files. This option is required only if the files are not located in the current folder.

- /tempdrive:drive_letter specifies which partition setup will use to store temporary files. This option is not recommended.

- /unattend is only useful for upgrades. All answers are decided based on information in the current operating system. No answer file is required.

- /unattend[num]:[answer_file] specifies the name of an answer file. Answer files are used to bypass the interactive questions asked of the user and can even be used to automate the setup process completely. The optional *num* parameter is used to specify the number of seconds between the time setup finishes copying the files and the time setup restarts.

- /udf:id[,UDF_file] specifies an ID in a uniqueness database file (UDF). A UDF makes changes to an answer file that varies from one machine to another. For example, you can specify computer names in a UDF. This allows a single answer file to be used for all systems on a network.

- /cmd:command_line specifies a command to be executed after setup has completed. This can be used to launch automated application setup routines to complete the installation.

- /copydir:folder_name copies a folder you create into the system folder. This option is generally used to copy drivers that are not part of the standard Windows 2000 distribution. This option can be used multiple times to copy multiple folders.

- /copysource:folder_name operates in much the same way as /copydir, but the folder is removed after the setup has completed. This option is for transferring additional setup files to the system.

■ /syspart:drive_letter is used to copy setup files to a partition of a hard disk and mark the partition as active. The hard disk can then be installed in another computer. When that computer is started, the next setup phase starts automatically. This option must be used with the /tempdrive:drive_letter option.

Deploying Large Sites

When installing fewer than 20 systems, manual installation is efficient. However, for larger networks, it is worth the administrator's time to automate as much of the setup as possible. One method of automation is the answer file. Using answer files is a complex topic and is described in more detail in the *Microsoft Windows 2000 Server Resource Kit* (Microsoft Press, 1999).

Another method of automating setups—remote installations—was described in Chapter 3. Remote installation is the most efficient way to perform a massive deployment of Windows 2000 Server.

Upgrade Paths

You can upgrade any of the following operating systems directly to Windows 2000:

■ Windows 95

■ Windows 98

■ Windows NT 3.51 SP5

■ Windows NT 4.0

Older operating systems, such as Windows NT 3.1, Windows NT 3.51, and Windows for Workgroups, will require either an upgrade to one of the systems on the previous list or a brand-new installation.

NOTE: · If you must perform a new installation for a user, consider configuring the system as dual-boot for a week so he or she can use the previous operating system if any problems arise with an application.

Whether you are creating a new installation or upgrading an existing system, the same installation options apply. You can choose to load the software from a network file server, from a local CD-ROM, or by using the remote installation features discussed in Chapter 3.

Setup Walk-Through

The manual setup routine will take you through a series of steps in a very wizardlike fashion. Make sure you have the necessary information gathered before you begin the setup routine. Here is what you'll be asked for:

- **Licensing Agreement** Be sure you have purchased a license for every instance of Windows 2000 you install.

- **Regional Settings** If you speak English and live in the United States, you can accept the defaults here. Otherwise, select the proper language and locale settings as discussed in Chapter 2.

- **Computer Name and Administrator Password** Both can be changed after setup has completed. Be sure to set an administrator password, or your machine will be vulnerable to attack as soon as the network starts.

- **Date and Time Settings** Choose your time zone. If this is the first operating system installed on the computer, you will need to set the time as well.

- **Network Settings** If you are using Dynamic Host Configuration Protocol (DHCP), select the default and your network settings will be automatically configured. If you must enter the settings manually, you should enter at a minimum an Internet Protocol (IP) address, subnet mask, and default gateway. If you are using DNS (Domain Name System) or Windows Internet Name Service (WINS), specify those servers as well.

- **Domain Settings** If you are joining a domain, you must have a user account that has rights to create a computer account in the domain.

- **Upgrade to NTFS** If you are not dual booting with an older operating system, you should upgrade your partitions to the NTFS file system. If you choose to skip this step now, you can always upgrade later.

- **Name and Organization**

- **Provide Upgrade Packs** Upgrade packs are used to modify applications to work with Windows 2000. Check with your software vendor to obtain an upgrade pack. They will not always be necessary—most software should run on Windows 2000 without modification.

Migrating to Windows 2000 Server

Most major Windows 2000 deployments will be upgrades from previous Windows operating systems. This section guides you through the entire migration process, breaking it down into six phases. Phase One, Streamlining, reduces the complexity of your network by cleaning up resources. Phase Two, Updating, improves the chances of a successful migration by upgrading current operating systems and applications to the latest patch versions. Phase Three, Planning, creates a detailed plan that will be followed for the remaining phases. Phase Four, Testing, validates the system architecture and flushes out any problems before they cause downtime. Deploying, Phase Five, is the actual installation of Windows 2000. Finally, in Phase Six, Determining Success (or Failure), you evaluate the work and determine whether you have succeeded.

Phase One: Streamlining

Make the migration as simple as possible by cleaning up your existing network and servers. This is good practice at any time, but it is particularly helpful when preparing to upgrade. Audit your user account database to ensure there are no duplicate or unused accounts. Clean unnecessary files off every server and desktop system, and make sure that all systems have plenty of free space.

If you have been putting off any hardware upgrades necessary to support your existing environment, perform them now. Windows 2000 Server is more demanding of hardware than Windows NT Server 4.0 is.

Phase Two: Updating

Windows 2000 Server is a major update from Windows NT Server 4.0, but many of the new features have been released as add-ons. Make your migration smoother by implementing these updated components on all of your servers several weeks before you plan to upgrade. In particular, make sure Windows NT Server 4.0 Option Pack (with Microsoft Internet Information Server 4.0 and Microsoft Transaction Server) and Windows NT 4.0 Service Pack 4 are installed.

> NOTE: Both Windows NT Server 4.0 Option Pack (with Microsoft Internet Information Server 4.0 and Transaction Server) and Windows NT 4.0 Service Pack 4 are available for free download from *http://www.microsoft.com*.

Your system's architecture might need to be revised. If you are using any network protocols besides TCP/IP, remove them. All other major network operating systems support TCP/IP, so compatibility is not an issue.

Next, make sure you are taking full advantage of the TCP/IP services included with Windows NT Server 4.0. Make sure you have WINS servers on your network and that all clients are configured to use them. Also, consider using DHCP; while it's not suited to all environments, you should take advantage of it if possible.

Implement a DNS structure and configure all client machines to use DNS. If you currently use UNIX for DNS services, migrate the servers to Windows NT for tighter integration with Active Directory. If you cannot migrate all DNS servers, create a separate subdomain that can be handled exclusively by Windows NT servers. Having a separate subdomain fits into the Active Directory architecture very well and limits the damage if problems occur during migration.

Windows 2000 networks do not require NetBIOS networking. To ease the transition from NetBIOS, make sure that all systems have a primary host name that matches their computer name. For example, if a server has the computer name KURT and a fully qualified domain name (FQDN) of *www.company.com*, give it an alias in the DNS database as kurt.company.com. After you have performed these updates to your network, you are ready to begin planning the migration.

Phase Three: Planning

Several important tasks must be completed before you begin updating systems. The tasks are as follows:

- Map out a system architecture.
- Determine a budget.
- Create a detailed task list.
- Specify a timeline.
- Identify human resource needs.

Creating a System Architecture

Windows 2000 has different architectural requirements than Windows NT 4.0. For example, your new architecture might not require multiple domains and so might need fewer domain controllers. Alternatively, you might need to add a DNS infrastructure, which would require purchasing additional hardware.

Take the time to create a diagram of the new architecture and itemize any necessary additional hardware and software. You will use this itemization when determining a budget and creating a task list.

Be sure each of your Windows 2000 systems meets these specifications:

- 166 MHz or higher Pentium-compatible microprocessor or Alpha CPU

- 32 MB RAM for Windows 2000 Professional; 64 MB RAM for Windows 2000 Server

- 2-GB hard disk with a minimum of 500 MB of free space

- VGA monitor and video card

- Keyboard and mouse

- A network card or CD-ROM to retrieve the setup files

Determining a Budget

Migrating all the systems on a network is a major undertaking. It is much better to specify a budget beforehand than to run out of money halfway through a project, so take some time to estimate costs and verify that the funds have been set aside. Several factors will contribute to the overall cost:

- **Hardware upgrades**   Any system that does not meet the hardware requirements for the new operating system must be upgraded. Be sure to include the cost of labor in the estimate.

- **New hardware**   If your new system architecture requires that additional systems be purchased, include the costs of the hardware and set-up in the budget.

- **Software upgrades**   This will vary depending on your organization's licensing scheme.

- **Overtime**   In most organizations, employees have a full schedule simply performing day-to-day tasks. Planning and executing a major upgrade will consume additional time that will cost the company money if it pays overtime.

Creating a Task List

Create a detailed list of discrete tasks that must be accomplished during the migration. Consider the following scenario: You are upgrading your Windows NT 4.0 domain to Windows 2000 Server and Active Directory. You plan to start the migration by upgrading the primary domain controller for your domain, SERVER-PDC. This system requires a processor upgrade to run Windows 2000 Server effectively. The task list you create might look like this:

1. Verify that a processor upgrade kit and Windows 2000 Server software are available.

2. Perform a full backup of SERVER-PDC.

3. Inform users that SERVER-PDC will be taken offline.

4. Synchronize all domain controllers.

5. Promote SERVER-PDC to primary domain controller.

6. Add the additional processor to SERVER-PDC.

7. Synchronize all domain controllers.

8. Promote SERVER-PDC back to the primary domain controller.

9. Upgrade SERVER-PDC to Windows 2000 Server.

10. Verify that everything is functioning correctly. If SERVER-PDC is not working correctly, remove the additional processor and restore from backup.

11. Inform users that SERVER-PDC is back online.

By specifying each required step, you reduce the chance that anything will be forgotten. It is easy to forget to make a backup before upgrading a system, but skipping this step can have disastrous results if the upgrade does not work properly. Make sure several people in the organization review the task list to verify that no steps have been omitted. For large networks, start by creating a higher-level task list and dividing the list among different administrators.

NOTE: Always have a rollback plan! If any step fails, you should have a way to restore services to their original state.

Specifying a Timeline

Once you have created the task list, determining a timeline is easy. Determine how many hours of work are required for each task. Be realistic—leave extra time for human error and unexpected delays. Think about which tasks can be performed at the same time and which can only be accomplished after other tasks are complete. If you have the resources, you can have people working simultaneously on different tasks.

Identifying Human Resource Needs

Depending on the size of your network, migrating to Windows 2000 Server can take several months. During the migration phase, personnel will have to dedicate part or all of their time to upgrade tasks. Assign each task from the task list to a specific administrator. If you do not have enough people to accomplish the tasks within the given timeline, consider hiring consultants or changing the timeline.

Once you have identified who will participate in the migration, make sure they have the proper skills. Everyone is new to Windows 2000, so everyone will require some training, self-study, or both.

Phase Four: Testing

In an ideal world, all software would work as expected. Every administrator knows that networking is *not* an ideal world, so take measures to detect problems early. While planning, allocate time for software testing. Set aside a system, and install Windows 2000 Server on it. Then layer on the network applications you use and verify that each of them continues to work exactly as it did with Windows NT 4.0. Connect to the server with a variety of clients, and verify that the clients and the applications still function.

You will almost certainly uncover a few problems. It is obviously preferable to identify them in the testing phase when they will not cause user downtime. Troubleshoot any problems you find, and work with the software vendor's support groups to resolve the more difficult problems.

If you are upgrading desktop systems, be sure to test each of the different hardware platforms that you use. It helps if you can verify that all of your systems are on the Windows 2000 Hardware Compatibility List, but performing a test install on surplus hardware is the most reliable way to identify hardware compatibility problems. If your plan includes user-guided automated installations, have a user walk through the installation process to verify that the documentation you have provided is clear and accurate.

NOTE: The most recent Hardware Compatibility List is at *http://www.microsoft.com/hwtest/hcl.*

Even a small flaw in your plan can cause a great deal of downtime for your users. Testing is an extremely important phase, and it can save your organization copious amounts of money. Do not allow this phase to be bypassed because of a short timeline. But do not spend so much time on testing that you waste resources. Except in very large migrations, it is neither necessary nor productive to test every permutation of software and hardware, client and server.

Once you have resolved any problems revealed by the testing process, you are ready to begin implementation.

Phase Five: Deploying

Your planning and testing efforts will pay off during the upgrade to Windows 2000. Small organizations with less than 50 clients and servers should migrate all systems at once. Plan to do the work after hours when it will cause the least downtime for users.

It is not practical to upgrade medium to large organizations in a single phase. Instead, start by migrating primary domain controllers to Windows 2000 Server. Leave a full week after the first systems have been upgraded before migrating the backup domain controllers.

By migrating servers in small numbers and allowing the updated servers to function in a production environment, you are performing a final stage of testing. After all the servers have been upgraded, migrate user systems one department at a time. By taking small steps, you limit the worst-case scenario to partial downtime rather than total downtime.

Phase Six: Determining Success (or Failure)

After you have completed each phase of your migration, perform a series of tests to validate functionality. Even if everything is working okay, be prepared for users to raise support issues. There are usually surprises when performing a major upgrade. Deal with problems as they arise, and be prepared for the worst-case scenario: rollback. If any postmigration problems are severe and cannot be quickly resolved, restore your systems from the most recent backup and return to the testing phase.

I hope that everything will go as planned. You, the users, and your organization will all benefit from the improvements offered by Windows 2000.

Summary

This chapter has introduced you to the Windows 2000 Server setup routine and the steps required to successfully migrate your network. Depending on the type of installation you are performing, you must choose among running setup directly from the network or a CD-ROM, automating the process, or using remote installation functionality. You must also decide whether to upgrade systems or to perform a clean install of the new operating system.

A successful migration requires careful planning. For large networks, a dedicated project manager should run the deployment. Even small networks require careful planning to stay within budget, stay on time, and keep lost productivity to a minimum.

GLOSSARY

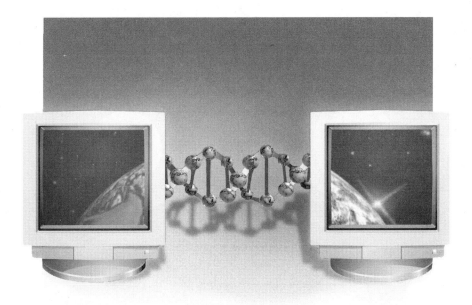

GLOSSARY

access control list   *See* ACL.

ACL   access control list. The permissions assigned to a resource that identify which users have access and which access attempts are logged. *See also* DACL, SACL.

ACPI   Advanced Configuration and Power Interface. A standard that allows the operating system to instruct the hardware to conserve power.

ACS   *See* QoS ACS.

Active Directory   A structure supported by Windows 2000 that lets any object on a network be tracked and located.

Active Directory Service Interface   *See* ADSI.

Active Server Pages   *See* ASP.

ADSI   Active Directory Service Interface. Allows applications to communicate with Active Directory.

Advanced Configuration and Power Interface   *See* ACPI.

Advanced Streaming Format   *See* ASF.

AH   Authentication Header. The component of IPSec that provides for authentication.

ASF   Advanced Streaming Format. The file type used for Windows Media Player streaming media presentations.

ASP   Active Server Pages. A script that is executed on the server before being transmitted to the user as an HTML page.

Authentication Header   *See* AH.

Bandwidth Allocation Protocol   *See* BAP.

BAP   Bandwidth Allocation Protocol. A component of Windows 2000 that allows multiple lines to be added to a dial-up connection as additional resources are required.

BOOTP   bootstrap protocol. A protocol for allocating IP information to clients upon startup. A predecessor of DHCP.

bootstrap protocol   *See* BOOTP.

CA   Certification Authority. An organization that validates the identity of a person or organization, and provides a unique key that can be used for authentication and encryption.

central processing unit   *See* CPU.

Certification Authority   *See* CA.

clustering   Combining multiple systems to act as a single, redundant system.

COM   Component Object Model. A development framework that allows applications to be broken into distinct parts.

Component Object Model   See COM.

CPU   central processing unit. The brains of a computer.

CPU throttling   A kernel-level capability used to limit the CPU cycles taken by a process. Within IIS, CPU throttling can stop a single virtual server from slowing an entire system.

DACL   discretionary access control list. Permissions assigned to an object that define which users have access.

DAV   Distributed Authoring and Versioning. An extension to HTTP/1.1 that allows robust control over a web server's content.

Dfs   distributed file system. A component of Windows 2000 Server that allows file shares to be maintained redundantly between multiple servers.

DHCP Dynamic Host Configuration Protocol. An Internet standard and a component of Windows 2000 Server that allows clients to be configured with an IP address and other IP information necessary for communication on the Internet.

discretionary access control list *See* DACL.

disk quota A limitation on a user's disk space.

distinguished name An entire LDAP name that uniquely identifies an object or container on a network. For example, the following distinguished name identifies the user Tony Northrup: /O=Internet/DC=COM/DC=Microsoft/DC=MSPress/CN=Users/CN=Tony Northrup

Distributed Authoring and Versioning *See* DAV.

distributed file system *See* Dfs.

DNS Domain Name System. A directory that allows names such as www.microsoft.com to be resolved to IP addresses.

Domain Name System *See* DNS.

Dynamic Host Configuration Protocol *See* DHCP.

EAP Extensible Authentication Protocol. A standard that allows for multiple methods of identifying users for dial-up communications.

EFS Encrypting File System. Allows data to be encrypted on the NTFS disk media, making it impossible for someone to bypass the operating system to retrieve the information.

EMA Enterprise Memory Architecture. Grants Windows 2000 Server the capability to address up to 64 GB of RAM, depending on the processor.

Encapsulating Security Payload *See* ESP.

Encrypting File System *See* EFS.

Enterprise Memory Architecture *See* EMA.

ESP   Encapsulating Security Payload. The component of IPSec that provides for encryption and validation.

Extensible Authentication Protocol   *See* EAP.

FAQ   frequently asked questions. A typical format for giving users introductory material on a topic.

FAT32   file allocation table-32. A file system supported for compatibility with Windows 98.

FAT   file allocation table. A file system supported for backward compatibility with MS-DOS, Windows 95, and Windows NT.

file allocation table-32   *See* FAT32.

file allocation table   *See* FAT.

forest   A group of Active Directory trees that trust each other.

Fortezza   A government security standard requiring long passwords to be stored on a separate piece of hardware, typically a credit card device.

frequently asked questions   *See* FAQ.

GB   gigabyte. Approximately one billion bytes (1,024 megabytes).

GC   global catalog. A directory used to identify any object on a network.

gigabyte   *See* GB.

global catalog   *See* GC.

Hierarchical Storage Management   *See* HSM.

HSM   Hierarchical Storage Management. A component of Windows 2000 Server that moves rarely needed data from local disks to cheaper media such as tapes. Data is automatically retrieved when needed.

HTML   Hypertext Markup Language. A standard for providing formatted documents on the Internet.

HTTP   Hypertext Transfer Protocol. A standard IETF Internet protocol used for the majority of World Wide Web communications.

Hypertext Markup Language   *See* HTML.

Hypertext Transfer Protocol   *See* HTTP.

IETF   Internet Engineering Task Force. The group responsible for creating Internet standards.

IGMP   Internet Group Management Protocol. A standard that enables multicasting to occur on the Internet.

IIS   Internet Information Services; Microsoft's web server product.

IntelliMirror   A suite of technologies to reduce total cost of ownership. IntelliMirror provides for redundant copies of data to be stored on both the client and server.

Internet Engineering Task Force   *See* IETF.

Internet Group Management Protocol   *See* IGMP.

Internet Information Services   *See* IIS.

Internet Protocol security   *See* IPSec.

Internet service provider   *See* ISP.

Internetwork Packet Exchange/Sequenced Packet Exchange   *See* IPX/SPX.

IPSec   Internet Protocol security. An IETF Internet standard for creating virtual private networks.

IP telephony   A technology that attempts to merge voice and data networks.

IPX/SPX   Internetwork Packet Exchange/Sequenced Packet Exchange. A legacy network protocol supported natively by NetWare.

ISP   Internet service provider. Typically ISPs provide dial-in, connectivity, and Web-hosting services.

ISSLOW　An IETF working group dedicated to creating a standard that allows streaming media data to operate on the same network as other data.

jitter　The rate at which network delay changes during the course of a session.

job object　A kernel-level object that tracks multiple processes working together to accomplish a single task.

Kerberos protocol　A standard for authenticating users on a network. Supported by Windows 2000 natively for all authentications.

kernel　The central part of Windows 2000; it has the highest rights to the hardware.

L2TP　Layer 2 Tunneling Protocol. A virtual private networking standard created by Microsoft, Cisco, Ascend, IBM, and 3Com.

latency　Delay that occurs as packets cross a network.

Layer 2 Tunneling Protocol　*See* L2TP.

LDAP　Lightweight Directory Access Protocol. A standard for naming and identifying objects on a network.

Lightweight Directory Access Protocol　*See* LDAP.

MB　megabyte. Approximately one million (1,048,576) bytes.

Microsoft Management Console　*See* MMC.

MMC　Microsoft Management Console. A framework for administrative tools in Windows 2000.

MPR　Multiprotocol Router. This term refers to the routing component of Windows 2000 Server.

MS-DOS　Microsoft Disk Operating System. A legacy Microsoft platform that hosts Windows 3.11 and earlier.

Multiprotocol Router　*See* MPR.

NAT network address translation. The process of transparently sending packets via proxy between an internal and external network.

Native Language Support *See* NLS.

NDIS network driver interface specification. The standard to which all Windows drivers are created.

NetBIOS The network standard for traditional Windows network communications.

network address translation *See* NAT.

network driver interface specification *See* NDIS.

NLS Native Language Support. Allows administrators to configure an operating system with locale-specific information.

NTFS file system A robust and scalable file system that allows for security and automatic recovery. The preferred file system for use with Windows 2000.

Open Shortest Path First *See* OSPF.

OSPF Open Shortest Path First. A link-state routing protocol used for exchanging network information between routers on an internet.

Plug and Play A standard that allows hardware and software to communicate and automatically configure themselves.

Point-to-Point Tunneling Protocol *See* PPTP.

PPTP Point-to-Point Tunneling Protocol. A standard for creating Windows virtual private networks.

private/public key security A security method that provides for encryption and authentication of one or both parties in a conversation.

processor accounting A kernel-level capability that tracks how much processor time each process uses. Useful for determining which IIS virtual servers consume the most CPU cycles.

QoS   Quality of Service. A standard that allows bandwidth and latency to be guaranteed by an application before network transmissions begin. QoS is critical for supporting streaming media on an internet.

QoS ACS   QoS Admission Control Service. A Quality of Service standard that allows administrators to control which users and groups can reserve bandwidth on a network.

QoS Admission Control Service   *See* QoS ACS.

Quality of Service   *See* QoS.

RAID   redundant array of independent disks. Allows multiple drives to act as a single, fast, redundant drive.

RAM   random access memory. The dynamic memory a computer uses for most operations.

random access memory   *See* RAM.

redundant array of independent disks   *See* RAID.

Remote Installation Services   *See* RIS.

Remote Storage   The actual process within Windows 2000 Server that performs the tasks necessary for hierarchical storage management.

Removable Storage   A component of Windows 2000 Server that tracks data stored on tapes and CDs.

replication   The process of duplicating files between multiple locations.

Request for Comments   *See* RFC.

Resource Reservation Protocol   *See* RSVP.

RFC   Request for Comments. An Internet standard maintained by the Internet Engineering Task Force.

RIP   Routing Information Protocol. A legacy distance vector routing protocol and a standard for communications between routers on a network.

RIS   Remote Installation Services. A component of Windows 2000 Server that allows clients' systems to be installed with little administrator interaction.

Routing And Remote Access   The component of Windows 2000 Server that allows for network communications over phone lines.

Routing Information Protocol   *See* RIP.

RSVP   Resource Reservation Protocol. An IETF Internet standard for providing Quality of Service to network applications.

SACL   system access control list. Specifies which actions are audited in Windows 2000.

script   A set of instructions that a system carries out designed to automate a specific task.

Security Support Provider Interface   *See* SSPI.

Server-Gated Cryptography   *See* SGC.

SGC   Server-Gated Cryptography. An extension of SSL (Secure Sockets Layer) that provides 128-bit encryption to banks that must communicate globally.

Single Instance Store   *See* SIS.

SIS   Single Instance Store. A service within Windows 2000 Server that saves space by eliminating duplicate files in IntelliMirror disk partitions.

Software Installation   New name of an MMC snap-in that was formerly called Application Deployment or Application Deployment Editor. A tool within Windows 2000 Server designed to help administrators deploy applications in Active Directory–enabled networks.

spin count   The number of times a process will attempt to access a shared resource before giving up and waiting. Spin count helps to improve the performance of multiprocessor systems.

SSPI   Security Support Provider Interface. A standard method for developers to build authentication into their applications.

subtree   A contiguous portion of an Active Directory domain.

system access control list   *See* SACL.

TAPI   Telephony Application Programming Interface. A component of Windows 2000 that allows applications to perform voice and telephone communications.

TCO   total cost of ownership. This term refers to the amount of money organizations spend on every aspect of managing computer networks.

TCP/IP   Transmission Control Protocol/Internet Protocol. The standard for network communications on the Internet.

Telephony Application Programming Interface   *See* TAPI.

total cost of ownership   *See* TCO.

tree   A single Active Directory domain.

tunnel   A conduit for transmitting VPN traffic.

Unicode   A standard that uses double-byte characters and can represent most common languages of the world.

user principal name   UPN. An e-mail address that provides a shortcut to an LDAP name. For example, northrup@ultranet.com could be the UPN to a much longer LDAP name.

virtual private network   *See* VPN.

virtual server   In IIS, a single Web site. It acts as if it were running on a dedicated system.

VPN   virtual private network. The process of sending data across a public network while keeping the data secret.

WAN   wide area network. A large network that extends beyond a single geographic area.

WDM   Windows Driver Model. A layer of Windows 98 and Windows 2000 that allows the two operating systems to use the same drivers.

wide area network   *See* WAN.

Windows Internet Name Service   *See* WINS.

Windows Management Instrumentation   *See* WMI.

Windows NT   A Microsoft operating system on which Windows 2000 was based.

Windows Script Host   *See* WSH.

Windows Terminal Services   *See* WTS.

WINS   Windows Internet Name Service. A component of Windows 2000 Server that provides NetBIOS name resolution. It allows client systems to locate servers on the network for traditional Windows communications.

wizard   A piece of software that guides the user through a complicated process by breaking the process into small steps.

WMI   Windows Management Instrumentation. A low-level interface that allows access to information about hardware.

WSH   Windows Script Host. A component of Windows 2000 that allows scripts to be executed in a variety of programming languages.

WTS   Windows Terminal Services. Allows multiple graphical sessions to be created on a single remote Windows 2000 Server.

Zero Administration for Windows   An initiative within Microsoft to provide tools that make administrative tasks extremely simple.

INDEX

Page numbers in italics refer to figures.

NUMBERS AND SYMBOLS

commercial CAs, trusting, 66

communications
capabilities of Microsoft Windows 2000 Server, 99
effect of latency on two-way, 93

Compaq NetFlex NICs, compatible with the RIS boot floppy, 36

compiled programs, compared to interpreted scripts, 53

Component Object Model. *See* COM (Component Object Model)

Component Services, 46

Component Services snap-in, 46, *46*

Compress Application Files option in IIS, 115

Compress Static Files option in IIS, 115

Computer Management MMC snap-in, 18, *18*

computer names
assigned to Windows systems, 124
basing by default on user names, 40
specifying in a UDF, 167

computer networks. *See* networks

console tree, 144. *See also* namespaces

container, 145

container objects, 145

contiguous subtree, 145

/copydir parameter in winnt32.exe, 167

/copysource parameter in winnt32.exe, 167

CPU (central processing unit), 180

CPU throttling, 4, 180

CreateObject call, 54

CryptoAPI, public-key algorithms available through, 20

cscript.exe, 53

custom development as a significant factor in TCO, 46

Custom Setup option within the Client Installation Wizard, 41

D

DACL (discretionary access control list), 180

data, mirroring between clients and servers, 33

data and voice networks, merging, 104

Data Encryption Standard (DES), 20

data link layer (layer 2) of the OSI model, 96

data network, 104

data warehouses, memory allocation for, 7

date and time settings for setup, 169

DAV (Distributed Authoring and Versioning), 116–17, 180

debug log file, creating during setup in winnt32.exe, 167

/debug parameter in winnt32.exe, 167

delegated administration, 146–47

Delegation Of Control wizard, assigning permission to objects, 146, *146*

Deploying phase of migration, 175

desktop systems
configuring from a central server, 11
powering on and booting without an operating system, 36

destination address, filtering packets based on, 78

Determining Success (or Failure) phase of migration, 170, 175

device configuration operations, supported by WMI, 51, *52*

device drivers. *See* drivers

Device Manager, 9, *10*

devices, configuring with management applications, 51, *52*

Dfs (Distributed file system), 180
architecture and features, 138–42
management of, 137–38, *138*

Dfs client software, 139

Dfs roots, 138
configuring multiple Windows 2000 Servers to share, 140
giving access to file servers in an enterprise, 139

Dfs root servers, hosting multiple in Active Directory, 139

Dfs trees, 24
creating, 138
levels of fail-over capabilities, 139
operating modes for, 141

Remote Access Service (RAS). *See* Routing and Remote Access

remote access users, validating, 101

Remote Authentication Dial-In User Service. *See* EAP-RADIUS

remote boot functionality, 9, 10–11

remote installations, 168

Remote Installation Service. *See* RIS (Remote Installation Service)

Remote Installation Service Setup Wizard, *38*, 38–39, *39*

Remote Storage, 27, 186

Removable Storage, 25, *26*, 28, 186

    controlling anywhere in the network, 25, *26*

    libraries in, 25

    scaling to enterprise proportions, 25

replay attacks, 84

replica schedules, synchronizing, 142

replication, 186

    for Active Directory, 150–52

    collisions, 151–52

    component of Dfs, 139

    between Dfs roots and between child nodes, 141–42, *142*

    relationships, configuring between servers, *128*

Request for Comments. *See* RFC (Request for Comments)

reservation process in RSVP, 94, *94*

resource records, stored in a DNS database, 123

Resource Reservation Protocol. *See* RSVP (Resource Reservation Protocol)

Restart a Previous Setup Attempt option within the Client Installation Wizard, 41

RESV (for reservation) message, 94

reverse-proxy, acting as, 87

revised location, 23

RFC (Request for Comments), 186

RFC 1001, 125

RFC 1002, 125

RFC 1058, 89

RFC 1112, 90

RFC 1122, 78

RFC 1123, 78

RFC 1323, 78

RFC 1510, 64

RFC 1541, 134

RFC 1542, 131

RFC 1583, 90

RFC 1723, 89

RFC 1823, 162

RFC 2018, 78

RFC 2131, 134

RFC 2136, 125, 148

RFC 2284, 102

/r:folder parameter with winnt.exe, 166

RIP (Routing Information Protocol), 89, 90, 186

RIS (Remote Installation Service), 186

    boot floppy, compatibility with network cards, 36

    components of, 36

    distributions, handling an object within Active Directory Users and Computers, *39*

    servers, 36

roaming profiles with Windows 95 and Windows NT, 33

roaming users, logging into any desktop, 135

rollback plan for migration, 173

rolling upgrade, 11

root OID, 156. *See also* Object Identifiers (OIDs)

ROUTE command-line interface, 88

routers

    causing latency, 92

    configuring to forward DHCP requests, 131

    exchanging information about networks, 89

routing, 86–92

Routing and Remote Access, 86, 99, 100–104, 187

    configuring and managing L2TP and PPTP, 83, *83*

    configuring static routing, 88, *88*

    enabling EAP, 101

    integrating into Active Directory, 100

About the Author

Tony Northrup, MCSE and Compac ASE, has been implementing Microsoft Windows NT networking solutions since the first generation of the product. He has worked as a consultant at some of the largest corporations in the United States, implementing Windows-based networks in a variety of environments. Tony lives in the Boston area and is currently responsible for network and system architectures at GTE Internetworking. He is also the author of *NT Network Plumbing* and co-author of *Networking Essentials Unleashed*.

The manuscript for this book was prepared and submitted to Microsoft Press in electronic form. Text files were prepared using Microsoft Word 97. Pages were composed by Microsoft Press using Adobe PageMaker 6.52 for Windows, with text in Galliard and display type in Helvetica. Composed pages were delivered to the printer as electronic prepress files.

Cover Graphic Designer
Tim Girvin Design, Inc.

Cover Illustrator
Tom Draper

Principal Graphic Artist
Rob Nance

Principal Compositor
Paula Gorelick

Principal Proofreader/Copy Editor
Roger LeBlanc

Indexer
Richard Shrout

Register Today!

Return this
Introducing Microsoft® Windows® 2000 Server
registration card today

Microsoft®Press
mspress.microsoft.com

OWNER REGISTRATION CARD   1-57231-875-9

Introducing Microsoft® Windows® 2000 Server

_____   _____   _____
FIRST NAME   MIDDLE INITIAL   LAST NAME

_____
INSTITUTION OR COMPANY NAME

_____
ADDRESS

_____

_____   _____   _____
CITY   STATE   ZIP

                                             (   )
_____   _____
E-MAIL ADDRESS   PHONE NUMBER

U.S. and Canada addresses only. Fill in information above and mail postage-free.
Please mail only the bottom half of this page.

For information about Microsoft Press®
products, visit our Web site at
mspress.microsoft.com

Microsoft·*Press*